Why *Life Changes* is

"Change is appallingly difficult. Anyone who has ever tried
to get into a smaller skirt size, stop biting her nails, or move
from corporate executive to entrepreneur can testify to that.
Since I've tried all three but only succeeded at becoming an
entrepreneur, I can speak to the elusive nature of change. We
all need help to push ourselves beyond the everyday expectations
of life. Thankfully, Jennifer Lewis-Hall has devoted her second
book to giving us the strength, the ideas, the motivation and the
strategy to make real, lasting change—and to deal with change
when it happens to us. Read this book, and you will be changed."

- Carol Evans, CEO and Founder, Working Mother Media

"Jennifer Lewis-Hall taps into our inner voice, turning the fear
of change into powerful resources to transform our lives. She gives
us the tools we need to deal with change in all aspects of our lives,
from broken relationships to lost jobs to dealing with divorce,
aging and newborn babies. Now is the time to change—
let *Life Changes* be the inspiration to help you do it."

- Tavis Smiley, Author, Television & Radio Host

"In this enlightening and inspirational volume, Jennifer slams on the
brakes in our minds, makes readers face the inevitability of change, and
then propels them to a new level of consciousness that she calls 'Power
Changes.' If you want to conquer fear of change, find your voice, achieve
your goals, and live your dreams, *Life Changes* is the book for you."

- Dr. Gwendolyn Goldsby Grant, Psychologist, Advice Columnist,
Essence Magazine, and author of *The Best Kind of Loving*

Broken relationships, lost jobs, aging parents, divorce, marriage,
newborn babies, growing older—all are incredible life-changing events.
Network journalist Jennifer Lewis-Hall shares her inspiring and practical
perspectives in her latest highly acclaimed work, *Life Changes: Using
the Power of Change to Transform Your Life*. Lewis-Hall, a prominent
television journalist, professionally certified life coach and international
motivational speaker, helps you tap into your inner voice to turn the fear
of change into a powerful resource for transforming your life.

Life
Changes

Using the Power
of Change to
Transform Your Life

Future Titles

The Journey Productions is proud to publish the
Life Changes™ series of books. Look for these future titles:

Life Changes: Using the Power of Change to Transform Your Career

Life Changes: Using the Power of Change to Transform Your Relationship

Life Changes: Using the Power of Change to Transform Your Spirit

and

365 Ways to Be Open to Grace: Daily Devotions for Living Well

Life
Changes

Using the Power
of Change to
Transform Your Life

JENNIFER LEWIS-HALL, BA, MSJ, CEC

The Journey Productions, LLC

Published by The Journey Productions, LLC
P.O. Box 135
Metuchen, New Jersey 08840
www.jenniferlewishall.com

The Journey Productions creates self-help, inspirational and motivational content for multimedia platforms.

Book Design: Tricia Breidenthal
Editor: Anna Cousins
Photos: Robert Milazzo

The author of this book does not provide or dispense any kind of medical advice or recommend the use of any technique as a form of treatment for physical or medical problems without the advice of a physician. The aim of the author is only to offer general information to assist you in your pursuit of positive living and spiritual well-being. The author and publisher pointedly and specifically disclaim any liability, risk or loss incurred as a consequence of directly or indirectly applying the concepts, information and tools described in the book. Names in the book are pseudonyms and have been changed where letters have been shared with readers.

Library of Congress Control Number: 2005908478

Hardcover ISBN 0-9773351-0-0
Tradepaper ISBN 0-9773351-1-9
Printed in USA
First Edition: April 2006

The Journey Productions, LLC
Metuchen, New Jersey 08840

Dedication

I dedicate this book to my kind, smart, handsome and insightful sons, who have given me an opportunity to grow, learn, listen and change my life in every way. I thank you, Joseph Arthur Hall II, for your quiet strength. And Joshua Brooks-Richardson Hall, I thank you for your honesty and determination. You are both a tremendous blessing to your father and me. It is our privilege to nurture you, love you and care for you and see you evolve into fine young men with each and every change that comes your way. Be blessed and continue to carry a message that all things are possible when you believe in the power that lies within you. No matter what changes in the world around you—always be true to yourself and let faith be your guiding light.

With all my love,

Mom

Acknowledgements

There are simply not enough ways to say thank you to my mother, Evelyn V. Lewis. She has been the sheer force behind me and beside me, never allowing me to give up on my dreams or give in to what she calls "stinking thinking"—that momentary lapse in judgment when you allow negativity to creep into your brain and convince you, falsely, of what you can't achieve. She has simply never tolerated it. Instead, this supreme angel in my life prefers to remind me to "keep a good thing going." Thank you, Mother, in every language in the universe, for all you have given me and all you have given up for me. I am so thankful that God gave you to me and bound our family together through both divine and difficult times. And to my brother Hunter and the entire Lewis family, all of you have helped me in so many ways with your undying encouragement, support and expertise.

To Anna Cousins, you are a gifted editor and wonderful to work with; and to my designer Tricia Breidenthal, your creativity flows abundantly. I thank you both for your patience and professionalism as *Life Changes* was being born.

It is also very important to acknowledge everyone who took time to be interviewed, contribute a letter or add to *Life Changes* in some way. Through your contributions each of us can be more empowered as we encounter changes every day.

Contents

Foreword *by Carmen Bazile*

It is not often that a foreword is prefaced by an explanation from the author. In this special case, however, I want to prepare readers to be moved in a powerful way by the words of minister, chef and culinary arts educator Carmen Bazile. She and I met on a national speaking tour and were both excited about delivering a positive message of health and well-being. However, an entirely different agenda emerged when I found out in the fall of 2005 that Bazile and her husband, natives of New Orleans, had been forced by the ravages of Hurricane Katrina to leave their home with just a bag of clothes and a beloved picture of her grandmother.

I had already approached a number of well-known people about writing this foreword. But then things changed. After her life-altering experience, it was Carmen Bazile's voice that I wanted people to hear as they embarked on their soul-searching journeys. I know of no better person to introduce you to the profound power of change and what it means—literally and figuratively—to get through life's storms. Carmen Bazile lost everything, except what is most important—her spirit.

I have met thousands of people in my life through my ministry and my work as a chef and culinary arts educator. But when I met Jennifer Lewis-Hall I had a strong feeling that she was more than just a speaker being paid to do an event. Jennifer had a presence that was years beyond her chronological age and alive with spiritual essence. I was filled with grace as she spoke to audiences about our ability to change, grow and develop, telling women and men throughout the nation that each day brought a new chance to improve and transform their lives.

In *Life Changes*, Jennifer tells you with conviction that wherever you've been, whatever is hurting you or wherever you hope to go, with each breath you are given an opportunity to begin again. These words ring true to me now more than ever. After losing all my worldly possessions, I've picked up the pieces of my life. I take a conscious breath at the beginning of each new day and I start again.

Experience has taught me that in order to survive change, we have to move beyond our fears and look to faith. We must take small steps in order to make big strides. I speak to women throughout the country, I know the Scripture and I live daily the words that help to heal a broken heart or depleted soul. *Life Changes* rings with a conviction that Jennifer and I share—that no matter what we are going through, we are all survivors. We are all blessed with more inner strength than we can ever know, a powerful force ready to help us move beyond pain, guilt, sorrow and anxiety.

Many of us are struggling more than ever to hold on to feelings of hope in the face of the tragedies of our times—terrorism, war, natural disasters. That's especially why I urge you to take Jennifer's advice to heart. She encourages us to lean on our inner strength and believe that even in times of tremendous uncertainty life is worth living. She asks us to seek out the things that are most important to us and embrace the little things that bring us joy—simple pleasures like time with family and friends, hearing your child's laughter or catching up with an old friend.

Jennifer and I share a love of butterflies. I'm not surprised. That's because there is a metamorphosis waiting to happen within each of us. As Jennifer says, no matter what is happening around us, we must believe that is it is never to late to change. *Life Changes* really is life-changing. I know. I lost all my worldly possessions, but not my spirit or my ability to live through incredible change.

Be Powerful, Be Well and Be Blessed,
Carmen Bazile
Minister, Chef & Culinary Arts Educator

Introduction

I am a woman who has grown to respect the saying that nothing worth having is easy. Rising in the field of journalism to work in network television, speaking to thousands of people throughout the United States, writing about ways to live well and enjoy the journey–all of this allows me to live my dreams. And while I am composed and natural in front of millions of viewers, none of this has been easy. There have been struggles, setbacks, disappointments and pain. And in so many ways I'm glad. I can say that because creating a life you love–one that is transformed with each and every change, no matter how hard that change is–is worth a fight. Through each struggle I've grown stronger and better prepared for the emotional mountains I have yet to climb. And as much as I have tried to resist change over the years, many of the most painful and dramatic changes are the ones that have taught me the greatest life lessons.

Take any stage of life and think about the lessons we learn through change. From the moment we're born, after being delivered from our mother's womb, we undergo tremendous external and internal changes. It happens the first time we open our eyes, when we take our first step, when we learn to speak. But instead of remaining fearless as we were as toddlers taking that first step–knowing all the while that we may fall–we quickly learn to become resistant and reluctant to experience new things.

Imagine for a moment what your life would look like if time stood still, if nothing was ever different from the day before. Imagine a world where you were never forced to experience new things or challenged by

adversity, or you never had a chance to discover something new by facing the unknown. It is often comfortable to stay exactly where we are, safe in a little cocoon, relying on the repetition of each day. The problem is that this existence means we are dying rather than living and stifled instead of growing. We are not vital when we don't experience, develop and grow—all components of the cycle of change.

I look forward to sharing with you the significant changes that have transformed my life, and letters from others who have learned that even in dark times, change can bring light. Know that change is the most powerful agent you have in living a life that is authentically *you.*

Think about how you are living and ask yourself if fear is holding you back from seeking a promotion, committing to a relationship, buying a home or moving to a new city. Not all the changes we encounter are dramatic. Many of us won't even try a new route to work or shop at a different grocery store because it involves change, and that makes us uncomfortable. I will help you explore what change really means, how it moves powerfully through our lives and how it can truly help us move closer to our goals, dreams and desires.

How to Use Your *Life Changes Journal*

If we have but one guarantee, it is that change is happening all around us. It's how we handle it and what we do with it that counts. As an important tool to help you examine the power of transition and transformation, I've created a special yearlong *Life Changes Journal* as a complement to this book. This will help you take a truthful look at yourself, how you view change and whether you're using the changes in your life effectively to live the way you really want to—rather than just settling for what comes your way every day. Your week-by-week *Life Changes Journal* will give you incredible insights into your strengths and will help you focus on lasting results for success.

1. Start using your journal as soon as you begin reading *Life Changes*. Throughout the book you'll find questions to answer and areas for self-exploration. As you write in your journal each week, think carefully about the questions you've read.

2. Don't rush the journaling process. Although time is a precious commodity, take your time with this journal and your thoughts. Allow yourself to think as you write so that you are making yourself and your goals a priority.

3. At the beginning of the *Life Changes Journal* is a set of general, open-ended questions. These are coaching questions designed to open your mind to the possibilities that change brings. Reread them as you write in your journal each week.

4. Continue to use your journal after you've finished reading *Life Changes*. Words of inspiration on each page of your *Life Changes Journal* remind you that *you* have the power to change your life. Use the questions at the beginning of the journal section to direct your thoughts. These questions will keep you on track for the positive changes you want to make over the course of a year.

The ability to change your life is in your hands. Be sincere and honest with yourself as you write in your journal each week. Then every few weeks, flip back through the pages and see how you can grow once you've opened yourself to the power of change.

Now let's begin on your personal journey to amazing *Life Changes*.

Change and the Big Picture

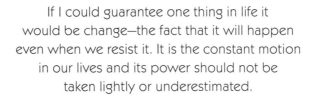

*If I could guarantee one thing in life it
would be change—the fact that it will happen
even when we resist it. It is the constant motion
in our lives and its power should not be
taken lightly or underestimated.*

What Is Change?

There are countless ways to understand the meaning of the word
'change' in our lives. Even dictionaries describe this simple term in many
different ways. Some of those definitions tell us that change occurs to
something when you "cause [it] to be different," or give it a "completely
different form or appearance," or put a fresh covering on it.* Seems simple, right? But don't be fooled. 'Change' is something that we've grown

---

* *The American Heritage College Dictionary*. Boston: Houghton Mifflin Company, 2000.

so accustomed to saying and hearing that we often take its meaning for granted. But we can see how this little word is actually a big deal when we talk about something as profound as changing the world for the benefit of our children, or something as personal and important to us as changing jobs to make a better life for our family.

Change is personal, change is powerful. Think about the magnitude of the word when we talk about changing ourselves. Your desire to change may come from wanting to improve yourself in some way from the inside out. I am certainly glad when I hear this from people, because at our very core there is always work to be done. Maybe it's about healing ourselves from a broken heart or replenishing our soul when a painful situation has left us feeling mentally, physically or spiritually depleted. Maybe it's just that deep-down desire to be kinder to ourselves, for ourselves—to treat ourselves better.

The simple dictionary definitions hint at new beginnings, chances to start over and improve. That's one key part of understanding change. The other very important element of the story–one that can't be found in the dictionary–is that the process of change is inevitable and continuous. Like so many things in life, the dictionary gives us some hard facts but doesn't interpret them for us or explain how they pertain to our lives. That is left up to you and I to do—and with the help of *Life Changes* we can begin to see the beauty of change in our lives and understand how this process–albeit an uncomfortable one at times–can be a revelation.

The impact that change has on each of us is incredible. The mere one-syllable word causes many of us to become fearful—at just the thought of doing something differently, trying something new or challenging ourselves in ways we never have before. The prospect of changing behaviors and thoughts that have stifled our progress should be something that we welcome. In casual conversations many people tell me they welcome change—but behind closed doors they admit they're terrified. They are afraid of the realization that what they are doing today could be altered dramatically in a mere twenty-four hours.

Things that sound easy to change can actually be the hardest things we've ever done, and because of this it's important to internalize the changes we want to make by journaling and writing down our goals. We say we're going to be more in touch with family or be more positive, but how many times have these regular conversations remained just that—

conversations, insignificant words that could have been powerful if we had backed up our talk with a timeline for change? I'm talking about living a life where our words become the framework for positive actions—a life in which we stop wishing for a better job or more time with our children or better bodies, and instead think about what we must do to spur the change for ourselves.

Why Change Is Profound

I can say with confidence that change has such an impact on our lives simply because it is a universal element that we must *all* confront. Each moment of the day we are consciously and subconsciously taking in new information and reprocessing old information in our brains. This constant influx and exchange has the ability to alter the way we view situations in our lives. Perhaps we have changed a belief or come to terms with something, or maybe we now disagree with someone because, as they tell us, we've "changed." The transformation is brought on by something that resonates with us or encourages us to consider a new perspective. When this happens it's a real breakthrough, isn't it! A belief or opinion that we held on to tightly–one that probably got in the way of our personal progress–suddenly appears completely different.

The idea that change can open doors for us is wonderful: when we allow ourselves to evolve we can see things that we had been blind to about ourselves, others and circumstances around us. It may be that we had been impeded by opinions that held us back from seeing another's perspective or kept us at odds with those we love. Separation set in as a result; only when we allow ourselves to grow can we see and feel things differently. That is why I'm so thankful that we have change in our lives—even though there are so many things that you and I want to hold on to.

When I speak in public about change I introduce it as part of a process that's essential to our daily lives. I ask people in the audience to take home one thought that resonates with them on that day; I tell them to put it squarely in the front of their minds and focus on it. Their job–and your job–is to work toward improving in that area throughout the year. I remind them, as I'm reminding you, that it's your choice to change, your choice to grow. And I can guarantee that if you do nothing to improve your life, absolutely nothing will happen. I know it's not easy—but nothing worth acquiring and preserving ever is.

If you think you're alone on this quest, think again. I have learned that tens of thousands of people in live audiences and millions on television all have something in common. Many tell me that a talk I gave, or something in my first book, inspired them to make the decision to change. We all have the innate desire to better manage the unexpected in our lives, and we all stand to benefit greatly by initiating positive transformations.

What kinds of transformations can result from our decision to grow? Change blesses us with the ability to:

become better partners, friends, neighbors;

become better parents and grandparents;

become better workers and employers;

become better savers;

become better dreamers;

become better listeners and communicators;

become better church members;

become better volunteers;

become better students;

become better at seeing life's little joys and laughing out loud;

become better at living in the moment;

become better at being thankful, kind and honest;

become better at planning for the future;

become better at forgiving ourselves and others;

become better at sharing knowledge and receiving wisdom from others;

become better at recognizing what really matters;

become better at reducing stress in our lives;

become better at appreciating different perspectives;

become better at living lives we love;

become better at taking care of ourselves.

Here are some real-life examples of how people just like you and me are making use of the power of change. These stories of transformation came from women I met during a speaking event in Georgia. They spoke to me about the importance of change in their lives and how they see it playing a powerful part in their future.

"I'm changing the way I see myself and the guilt I have over getting a divorce. My husband cheated on me for five years and I tried everything to keep our marriage together, but I finally decided to leave. I set out to get an apartment and the day I started looking I ended up with a house. It's hard, but I'm healing and I've forgiven him. I'm moving on."

"I'm changing careers and leaving corporate America as a senior executive to start my own business. It's time to branch out. What's the worst thing that could happen? I've been thinking about it for years and I need to try this now before it's too late."

"I'm changing the way I use my time—instead of wasting it, I'm going to use it to accomplish some of the goals that I have set for myself this year."

"I'm changing the way I eat. This is my year to get healthy."

"I'm changing my mind about going back to school. I thought it was something that I couldn't do. Now I know I have to make time for it if I'm going to make progress."

"I'm changing my spiritual focus. I heard the word today and I know that I have to make sure I go back to church. It is something that has been missing in my life."

"I'm changing the way that I've been trying to motivate my daughter. She's been down after dealing with a medical condition that caused her to temporarily lose her eyesight. I realize that she is stronger and more confident than anybody I know."

"I'm changing my approach when it comes to dealing with my aging parents. My mother suffered a series of minor strokes that caused her to have some memory loss. My dad doesn't want to move closer to me but I realize that I need to come up with an action plan in case something else happens."

"I'm changing the way I live and allowing myself to enjoy each and every day with my family. I thought my life was over after a debilitating back problem that caused me to become addicted to powerful painkillers. My mother helped me to come out of that addiction. It has been a slow and painful process but I am so thankful and feel good about my life now."

"I'm changing the way I see myself. I am 53 years old and this is my time! It's my time to live my life the way I want to, and to share the knowledge that I have with other women in my church—to let them know that they are worthy too."

Self-Discovery Through Change

If you examine the comments from the women who talked about a life-changing event or a vision for the future, you'll notice a key factor. The change they discuss fits into one of two categories: voluntary change and involuntary change. When an illness or disease develops in our bodies, involuntary change comes into play—it happens whether we like it or not. On the other hand, when we choose to get divorced or adopt a child we bring voluntary change into our lives.

The story of the young woman who lost her sight temporarily is an interesting one because it involves both kinds of change. While the mother who attended my talk could decide how to motivate and support her daughter through a difficult period, the daughter herself had no control over the initial life-changing event of losing her sight. But her story illustrates an essential point: even when we can't control the forces of change, we *can* decide how to adjust to and deal with new circumstances.

The young woman was in her early twenties at the time and going through a whirlwind of difficult challenges. The episode took a toll on her confidence and prompted her to leave college. She became depressed and felt a need to rethink her goals; she wondered whether she could ever be successful or achieve her dreams. Of course, the answer was a resounding 'yes'—but the success she yearned for would require her to adapt to a new and different situation.

Ultimately the positive potential of this change was far greater than the initial fear, sadness and anxiety it presented. After the young woman regained her sight, she began to focus on what she wanted to do with her life and decided to enter cosmetology school. She overcame her trauma and made a conscious decision to *live* in the fullest sense of the word— by starting a new career and moving beyond the sadness and fear that plagued her. She transformed her life in a powerful way in the midst of a very difficult change.

We commonly characterize change as either good or bad. However, it's often the so-called "bad" changes that have the potential to trigger the most dramatic improvements in our lives. I have never heard anyone say, "I'd like to go through something bad in order to feel good." However, when change happens–particularly change that affects our health, job status or lifestyle–we begin to pay close attention. We are forced into careful thought about how to deal with new circumstances. This is where the idea of discovery comes into play.

Consider this example. If you were to find out that you were in danger of being laid off or fired, your initial anxiety and fear might be followed by a new appreciation for your job—even if you didn't like it much to begin with. The fear that you wouldn't be able to support your-self or your family would make you want to hold on tightly. A multitude of worries would pop into your head: Will I lose my house and car too? What about my health insurance? These anxious thoughts are inevitable. But once your employer's cost-cutting axe fell and it was clear that your job was going to be eliminated, how would you actually handle it? How would you move from abstract worry to practical action?

Even though it's not something we like to think about, this type of unwelcome occurrence can often be life-changing in a positive way. Los-ing a job forces us to think about our value as an employee or manager. It forces us to take a close look at our skills and reexamine our resume. It pushes us to think about what we want to do rather than mechanically doing what we have been given to do. For many people this process leads to deep self-discovery: all of a sudden we're thinking about what we're good at, what our gifts are and what our deeper desires are.

Inertia is a powerful force—many of us probably wouldn't choose to change unless it became absolutely necessary. We allow ourselves to languish in a position because it's "okay" or pays us a "decent" amount of money and lets us "get by." I often say God has a funny way of shaking things up, whether it's at work or at home or anywhere else, in order to help us see the possibilities that await us. We all know the old saying, "If it ain't broke, don't fix it." However, there comes a time when we have to reevaluate our position—perhaps we've peaked on the job or have failed to grow in a relationship—and we have to admit to ourselves that maintaining the status quo is leading us in circles.

Allow change to shake things up in your life, to show you what you may be missing. You know how a snow globe needs to be shaken in order to reveal the snowflakes that have fallen to the bottom. Our lives are the same way: from time to time we must be shaken in order to see the beauty that otherwise remains hidden.

Changing Careers—My Personal Journey

This is a very personal issue for me because I would not have rethought or diverged from my own successful career in network television unless I had felt that there was something more desirable at that point in my life. The transformation began as I was thinking seriously about whether to renew one of my television contracts. It was a whirlwind period of pronounced change.

My career had hit another new peak—one that went hand-in-hand with new challenges and greater demands on my time. At the same moment my children were flourishing, expanding and growing, both mentally and physically, but they quietly yearned to have one of their parents close at hand. In my mind, this onslaught of change meant that important decisions would have to be made—and quickly. There wasn't time to think about another three years of working 60- and 70-hour weeks. I loved what I did, but my life was evolving. I wanted to evolve with it, rather than look back someday and wonder where that precious commodity—time—had gone.

As I sat in meetings with network executives discussing the next steps for my career, I thought to myself that if I was going to keep my professional steam going at such a determined pace, it would have to be worth it. 'Worth it' meant a schedule that would allow personal changes to work with the professional ones—added responsibilities on the job, a more structured schedule that would allow me to maintain some sanity. I had put in the time to have my own show, schedule and time slot on the air. I was a team player. But I was haunted by a persistent question: What would I have to give up personally in order to make those professional gains?

I thought about my goals and the expectations within the industry, and I had to ask whether my vision for myself aligned with the vision the networks held for me. By industry standards, key players are expected to deliver consistently high ratings and big exclusives. But after these years in the business, my inner voice was screaming out to me that there was more. In my heart there was a deep desire not only to deliver news and inform thousands of people daily, but also to help them improve their lives. Therein lay the difference.

It was when I expressed these thoughts in meetings that my vision for myself became truly clear. At that point I knew it was up to me to change my professional life in order to build on the career that I had loved. Doing that would mean changing my professional status and taking a huge leap of faith. In order to be successful I had to believe that I had a message, that I was blessed with the ability to tell it, and that communicating that message was part of my purpose on this earth.

However inspiring this personal vision was, the changes it would require were intimidating. I can't say that I truly embraced the idea at first. The safe option was to continue doing exactly what I was doing and what I had loved for so long—television reporting. Pursuing my new vision was much less safe, and many said it was unthinkable—to carve out another niche in the television and publishing industries as a contributor and producer, while also helping people directly as a life coach.

Many factors came into play as I weighed my choices. There were important family considerations: my children would be heading into elementary and middle school, and my husband was taking on added responsibilities as the result of a corporate merger. Then there were the challenges of starting out in a new profession. I knew that going out on my own would require all the skills I had learned in my career, including many I had picked up along the way in marketing, publicity and book-keeping. I would have to form my own business and build on what I knew. In between throwing in a load of laundry and doing homework I'd write, interview and produce stories.

I was told I was crazy, that I should give it time before making any serious decisions, and that I shouldn't abandon a good position for the sudden whim of wanting to be an entrepreneur. While I thought about my plans for several months, my decision-making went in stages. Initially I decided that I could ride out the career I had and maintain the status quo. Then, out of the blue, something inside me changed. Just when I had settled into the idea that I could do this for three more years, keep it fresh, maintain a good home life and keep up the daily commute up and down the highway, it occurred to me that I needed to be clear with myself about *why* I was content to stay in this situation. Was it fear? Was it a need for security? Was it the money? Which feeling did I crave more—the comfort of remaining where I was, or the excitement of paving my own way?

The answer to my dilemma didn't come solely from within—it came through me as the result of a meeting with a television executive. Just when I had accepted the path of maintaining the status quo, I learned that my vision for my future in the career did not match the vision that this executive had for me. Now the answer was undeniable: I couldn't keep up the status quo and be pleased with myself and my decisions. It wasn't okay to stop growing or facing new challenges and opportunities. These thoughts went through me like a lightning bolt. "I get it, God," I said silently. "You can hit me over the head once but you don't have to do it twice." (At least, not in one day!) It was at that moment that I decided not to let anyone else define me. I realized that it was *my* job to be proactive about the changes in my life.

So I took that leap of faith that I often talk about and, blessedly, people responded. Viewers followed my new path on television, sent notes and e-mails and sought out my skills as a coach. Others simply but powerfully encouraged me on my new journey.

Change is power, whether you like it or not. This change was going to happen for me because God had a bigger plan. I had information but not all the information, so to speak. So while I thought I was in control of all things involving my career and my life, I wasn't entirely then, and I'm not now.

What I thought I wanted really was what was best at that time—and that was proven in a powerful way a year after I set out on my own. The first year was extremely difficult. Managing the finances, making new and old contacts, maintaining a home office *and* managing the household was a whole new challenge. Sometimes there was visible progress and sometimes there wasn't. But all along I believed that the right doors were being closed and the appropriate doors opened.

Perhaps I should have listened to an Evangelical religious leader who had a vision for me many years ago. I was hosting an event as a favor for a professional colleague whose church was having its annual dinner. Near the end of the evening a very tall and confident-looking man–the bishop–stood behind the podium. I thought he would close out the dinner with a prayer and words of thanks, but instead he began to prophesy what he saw for the future. Growing up as a member of the Catholic and Episcopal faiths this was a bit different for me. But of course I was intrigued and glad to listen—that is, until a key part of that prophecy involved me.

The bishop was telling the group of about two hundred people that someone in the room would have a very special path to follow and it would allow them to help others enhance their lives. To my surprise, that "someone" was me. This path, as he explained it, would be far greater and more significant than the journey I was already on. It made me a bit uncomfortable, as I had been singled out in such a dramatic way, but it felt incredibly inviting at the same time. As hundreds of eyes were fixed on me, I experienced a sense of euphoria that I'd never felt before.

Now speaking directly to me, he said in a resonating tone that one door would close but another one would open, revealing a world of limitless possibilities for me. He told me in front of this large gathering (who had yet to touch their desserts!) that I needn't fear a thing, because my future would be filled with great and abundant possibilities.

Fine, I thought. Thanks. What could possibly be wrong with abundant and new opportunities—except for the fact that if he was right, it would involve the dreaded "C" word, *change*.

What did he see that I didn't see, and how could he see this? Wouldn't it have been easier just to wish me well and say how proud he was of me?

But as I've learned, there was a lot of truth to that revelation, no matter what religion you are. In order to move on to something far more rewarding I would have to change. My current situation was great, but was it the best thing for me during this time of transition in my life?

Needless to say, years later that prophecy has been proven true in even the most subtle of ways. Perhaps you could say it's a self-fulfilling prophecy—one that comes to fruition because you begin to believe it. However, I think the thought I held onto most was that change is coming whether I like it or not, and that it can have a profound and positive impact on my life. This is part of the "discovery" that happens when we embrace change rather than deny it.

Chapter 2

Confronting Change and Fighting Fear

"Change is the best teacher"

Lydia,* a college advisor, explains in this letter how change is working in her life. Although it hasn't been an easy process, it has been one of the most valuable lessons she has ever learned —about herself and what she has the ability to achieve.

In most of our lives, change is sometimes welcomed and sometimes not. Changes are constant and inevitable. I ask myself, do I have a fear of change? Do I embrace change? How do I feel about change? I feel that regardless of the change, positive or negative, it is up to the individual to understand what they are experiencing and focus on the positive outcomes. At some point in time change will stare you in the face. More importantly change will bring you through the cycle of transition to transformation many times over.

---

* All names have been changed.

One major change that happened in my life was truly a result of changes in my interpersonal relationships with family, friends and the love of my life. I would say that I employed both good and poor skills in dealing with this particular experience. I found myself in a two-year relationship with a person who I feel is the love of my life. During this relationship, I went through a period of transformation. I grew to understand who I am and what my dislikes are and get in touch with my emotions. These were some of the good skills I used to deal with change. I grew a lot and the person I was spending my life with was helping.

Taking a step back, my fear of change was strongest when I was coming out of a five-year abusive relationship. I was living in the state of Florida with no family and not many friends. The man I was engaged to and living with at that time was the center of my world. During our engagement, a couple of months before the end of our relationship…he woke me up one morning and simply told me he could not marry me. Change was staring me in the face! I was going to have to deal with transition to get to a level of transformation. I needed to embrace change whether I wanted to or not. I needed to find a place to live—this was change. I needed to learn to be alone again—this was change. I needed to understand I was not going to marry the individual I wanted to—this was change. All of this change led me to be more in touch with myself and learn to be alone and independent, and taught me that I could love again. Some of the destructive parts of this change were depression and suicidal thoughts. Again, I was able to embrace the situation for what it was and get help. Through this change my transformation was to persevere and complete my master's degree and start a doctorate and continue with my personal goals. It taught me how to handle change; however, the face of change would soon present itself to me once again.

My next relationship, the one I mentioned earlier, taught me how to deal with change. This was with my last boyfriend of two years. We had a lovely relationship, a lot different from the last. It was not abusive and allowed me to learn a lot about myself. Towards the end of this relationship things were rocky and did not work out. The man I loved threw me out of his house and I was left with nowhere to go. I needed to find a new place to live and maintain my job and studies. I never thought I would find myself in this position again. My transformation happened when I realized that I had to deal with a similar situation from my previous relationship. However, this experience taught me that others will sometimes just simply disappoint you. The positive outcome of this is that I have established myself professionally and financially and focused more on myself. Things like buying that first house, focusing on career…all of these things with almost no support system. No family around, no family support and very few friends.

The power of change will stare you in the face and teach you to do some amazing things. Many lessons were learned through these experiences. I'm trying to learn how I can understand the transition, not be afraid of it and allow it to work within myself. Ultimately I look forward to transformation because I always look to the positive.

Lydia, college advisor

Often when we think of change we think of being forced into something we don't want, don't accept or don't believe will benefit us. But Lydia has "seen the light." The light is a feeling of relief—as if you've been trapped in a dark basement and then, suddenly, you see a thin glimmer of light seeping under the door. The light is that breath you exhale that allows you to feel that everything is going to be all right. For Lydia it was a calm after the storm. She had been through an abusive relationship, one where her trust in the heart and the actions of her partner was betrayed and she was hurt to the very core.

So where is the beauty in this difficult situation? Looking again at an excerpt of Lydia's letter, we see that she grew to know and tap into her own strengths—even after a second relationship failed too:

> "My transformation happened when I realized that I had to deal with a similar situation from my previous relationship. However, this experience taught me that others will sometimes just simply disappoint you. The positive outcome of this is that I have established myself professionally and financially and focused more on myself."

Embracing Change

Lydia's story is one of change and transformation that grew out of self-reliance. In order for this change to take effect, she had to make an important discovery: that the relationships she was in were not moving her forward—they were hurting her. It would only be so long before the problems in her personal life spilled over into her professional life and surrounding relationships.

Whether she was ready for transformation or not, circumstances were altering all around her. Change is inevitable; the key is to direct the change yourself before it wreaks havoc in your life.

Let's take a moment to revisit what change is and why it's so important. At the beginning of this book I explained that change is a constant motion in our lives. Here are more thoughts to add to that philosophy:

Change is an agent for transforming our lives in a positive way.

Change is so profoundly important because it pushes us to achieve things many of us wouldn't readily do on our own.

Now I want you to understand two other very important concepts. One of these is what I call "power changes."

Power changes are changes that propel you to a new level of awareness, help you make your mark, help you achieve a goal, help you free yourself from a negative situation.

As a life coach I get to help people use power changes in very effective ways. A number of people I coach are interested in starting their own businesses, mostly to allow themselves more free time. What might be the power change for someone seeking this kind of freedom? Rarely is it to quit an existing job and take out a ton of loans. Instead, the real lasting power change is to explore what needs to happen in stages to make this change not only happen, but happen with a high level of success. The solution in this example is to alter the way you currently operate to allow more time to cultivate ideas, make a business plan, and do some market research—before entirely changing your career or income stream.

If you know someone who likes to gossip and share juicy information at the PTA meeting or in church (and probably gossips about you, too, when you're not around), how about making a power change by sitting in a different seat or by simply not entertaining the conversation. Think about whether this ongoing gossip is the best use of your time.

There are as many ways to make power changes as there are people. What power changes can *you* make?

The Phases of Change

The next important concept is one worth describing in detail, and that's what I call "Phases of Change." Here are the key phases of change and then some important questions you should ask yourself about how change manifests itself for you. Use your knowledge of the phases I've defined for you to become proactive about the changes in your own life.

JENNIFER'S PHASES OF CHANGE

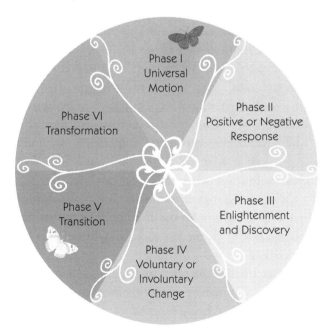

Phase I–Universal Motion

Your understanding of each of these phases, and your ability to move through them, is vital to your success in dealing with change. I call Phase I Universal Motion because it encompasses all of the energy that we give off and take in. It is the flow of events and issues that impact us whether we acknowledge them or not. Expanding your awareness of what is happening around you will allow you to act first or react quickly when you sense that a change is underway.

Phase II–Positive or Negative Response

In Phase II you get a chance to see how the energy that moves constantly around you is manifested in an emotional way. For example, if you're undergoing change at work that requires you to take on added responsibilities, this may excite you or cause a tremendous amount of anxiety. The important part of this phase is knowing that you have choices. How will you handle the news that more is going to be expected of you at work—or that you'll have to put off your plans to buy a new car or a new house or go back to school? This phase all boils down to one thing: how you react to the change at hand.

When I decided to make that big career move, the change was happening well before I was aware of it. I was being prepared all along by getting national and international recognition on television and in the publishing field, and by writing speeches on subjects ranging from career success on Wall Street to commencement addresses at major universities. At first I was puzzled: at each and every step I was being asked to push myself even harder, to learn new things at an extremely fast pace, and to ramp up my ability to digest and comprehend difficult information—all with a family that was waiting for me at home. The greater plan for my life was unfolding, but I was the last to know—or more accurately, the last to acknowledge it.

The key is that I had to be open to it. And so do you. With every speech that kept me up at night, and every show I woke up to prepare for at two in the morning, I was being prepped for the road ahead. I remember fighting this feeling of growing into a new dimension of my career.

After all, it would take even more work to learn something new. I had grown comfortable with what I was, and that was fine.

A negative response to change can take the form of immobility—doing nothing, hoping the change will simply disappear. Or, we can sink further into a negative mode by pitying ourselves or believing that we are powerless when it comes to modifying our own lives, goals, dreams and behaviors.

But what if there is a greater plan for you than you realize? When I finally stopped resisting change, new opportunities literally opened up right in front of me. It's not that these opportunities weren't there all along—the difference was that I was finally open to receiving them, open to the blessings that were mine to have.

Ask yourself, how open am I to what awaits me, and am I ready to receive it when it comes? Am I ready to embrace the change? I know in my heart that there is value there for you as you seek to embrace the transitions in your own life.

Phase III—Enlightenment and Discovery

As we say in television, Phase II is the perfect segue into what follows it. You are now ready to enter Phase III because you have a greater awareness that a change is taking place, and you know that you have a tremendous amount of control over your own destiny. You can feel the enlightenment and the discovery within you because you are more in control. When you are aware that change is taking place, acknowledging it and asking yourself how you feel about it is a natural process of discovery. This is a very beautiful and empowering part of the process of embracing change. Allow yourself to fully reap the benefits of this phase—to see the greater successes in your life that are brought about by change.

Phase IV—Voluntary and Involuntary Change

Through all the challenges in my own life it has been very helpful for me to recognize when I have evoked change and when change has spiritually resonated around, beneath and through me. The beauty of being alert to a voluntary change–such as an engagement, childbirth or a significant move–is that it allows us to prepare our total bodies mentally, physically and spiritually.

When change is involuntary, the same benefits of preparation present themselves. But there are other qualities that each of us has inside and must draw upon when change is involuntary. These qualities include perseverance and persistence. Again, involuntary change is change that we didn't knowingly initiate or had no outward control over, such as the death of a friend or loved one, an accident or corporate downsizing. These are just a few examples—there are as many voluntary and involuntary changes are there are people in the universe.

Phase IV–Transition

At this point you have some important knowledge about the changes that you want in your life, and you are more attuned to other changes that are happening. With this awareness you are better able to structure and create a life that you can deal with, appreciate and love. This transition is a vital part of our lifelong development because it's a pivot point to transforming our lives in some way.

Think back to Lydia, the woman who wrote to me about the difficult relationships that had failed in her eyes. Rather than failure, I see success and triumph: she was able to transition and transform her life by developing a deep understanding of herself, her desires and her goals. These relationships were clearly painful, but in the end she was able to see what she did not want and how she did not want to be treated.

Perhaps you have encountered roadblocks that have gotten in your way of achieving a particular goal. These barriers to success can be very clear, or they can be masked by what appears to be failure. In each case, circumstances may be telling you that your persistence will pay off, despite setbacks, and that the time has to be right for you to take that next step. The so-called failed attempts at landing the right job or buying a home may in fact mean that a better home–or one that's less expensive and less of a burden on tight finances–is on the horizon.

The transition phase means that big things are about to happen. If you allow yourself to fully experience change, you will find that you can physically feel when transition is underway. It feels like intense energy or momentum building in your life. How many times have you felt this? If it's relationships you're concentrating on, perhaps you're going out more regularly, meeting nicer people and getting closer to the type of relationship you want. Know that transition is an essential part of the process, leading you closer to your goals—even when you encounter difficult times or unanticipated setbacks.

Phase V–Transformation

At first glance the transformation phase could be viewed as the "unveiling" in a television makeover. You've seen the faces and bodies of the plastic surgery patients who have just gotten the makeover of a lifetime, from their eyelids to their teeth right on down to their ankles. The major difference here is that you've got to fix the inside first and *then* move to the outside forces in order to really see yourself as a success in the transformation phase. Only through this inside-out approach will you see its effects manifested for the long term.

In the transformation phase my clients experience what I call the "buy-in." This means that they are changing something in their lives not because they've been told to do so since they were children, or because their self-worth is caught up in how others view them, or because it's the popular thing to do. The buy-in is when you and I know why we're changing something in our lives, we believe it is best for us, and we are willing to do the work to make it happen. It's something you do because you feel it's right and you are truly committed to it.

Arriving at the point of transformation is incredibly special because it represents your hard work and dedication. It's proof that you've put in the time and effort to move a roadblock in your life, or you've stepped up your commitment to modifying how you're living, or you've been able to get through something very difficult or even debilitating—illness, divorce, abuse.

Reaching the transformation phase doesn't mean that you stop growing, that you have all the answers or that you aren't going to face new and fresh challenges in your life. Its strength is in the experiences you went through to get there, and your understanding of how your transformation has helped you. The power of transformation lies in what you learn from it.

Know that relatively small and simple acts have the most profound impact on us over time. Suppose the transformation you desire is to stop living your life as a junk-food junkie and begin eating healthy snacks. That's a big deal—you are improving your health radically in the long run, and for many people these preventative measures could end up prolonging, if not saving, their lives. Maybe solid relationships have been difficult for you to achieve without confusion, anger and regret. As a coach I would ask you where you'd like to see yourself in three months, six months, a year. If you could be transformed in some way pertaining to your relationships, what would you want to see? Do you envision a kinder person, a more compassionate person, a more loving, honest and open person?

When you have achieved a positive transformation, one that you are proud of and that feeds your soul, pat yourself on the back—but realize that the cycles of change continue. It's how you deal with them that is important.

Use your *Life Changes Journal* to jot down where you are with regard to the phases of change. Ask yourself what kinds of energy and circumstances surround you. Have you had a positive or negative response, and why? What have you learned, discovered or been enlightened by? Are these changes voluntary or involuntary? What is the transition you can see and what is the ultimate transformation for you? Refer back to each of the phases as you write.

To change is... to go from one phase to another,
to adapt, to evolve, to modify, to grow.

Transition is... passage from one state, activity or place to another.

Transformation is... a marked change in nature,
appearance or condition, usually for the better.

Open up to change. As you write in your *Life Changes Journal* this week, the questions below will help you explore the change, transition and transformation in your life.

Think about relationships, finances, spirituality, career, loss, diet and fitness—all kinds of personal and professional transformation. Most of us have a hard time with changes. When have you experienced this in your life? How has change affected you? What was the change and how did you handle it, whether poorly or with great skill?

1. What is it about change that scares you most? Why? Think of a specific instance of change that was difficult for you. What lessons did you learn from the experience and how has it helped to shape your thoughts?

2. When have you been in what I call a "cycle of change"? Think about your progress from one phase of the cycle to the next. Describe your experiences of success and challenge at each step. How did you ultimately grow, personally or professionally?

3. Change is inevitable. Rather than fear it, how can you allow it to enhance your life? What does the power of change mean to you?

Chapter 3

Instruments of Change

Icall this chapter "Instruments of Change" for a specific reason. An instrument–in addition to being something we use to make beautiful music–is also an implement or a tool we use to get something done. There are countless tools we can use to facilitate changes in our lives. These tools come into play when we change the environment where we live or work, change a relationship with a friend or co-worker, change a personal goal or opinion.

The actual instrument of change could be a person who introduces you to a new point of view, for example, or it could be an event. Typically we feel forced into using such tools when times are desperate—when we're caught in the middle of company layoffs, serious illness or other major life events. All of a sudden we have a heightened awareness of possibilities and opportunities in our lives.

But wouldn't it be great to see these possibilities *before* hard times came knocking? When we prepare for change–even in the worst of times–we're better off than when we're caught with our guard down. Give some thought to instruments of change in your own life. What can you do to move toward successful change? Here are a few ideas to get you started.

- Organize your surroundings. This can mean your home office, your workshop, your bedroom, an overstuffed closet—any spot that could benefit from some attention. This will help improve your focus and clarity.

- Set goals using a timeline. Make 3-month, 6-month and one-year goal charts.

- Daydream! Allow yourself some time to think about things you'd like to do, and consider how they could change your life in a positive way.

- Try something new. Growth comes with every internal and external change that's recognized and honored. Expand your horizon—try hiking, try a new kind of food, take an exercise or adult education class.

- Make a difference. When you're troubled by world events, think about what you can do to make a positive change—volunteer, hold a fundraiser or help someone in need.

- Write your thoughts down. Journaling is one of the most powerful tools we have in making positive changes.

Many of us know someone whose company went through rounds of layoffs, but when their own division was finally hit they said they "hadn't seen it coming." We've seen the headlines about the changing economy and job market—the so-called "wave of corporate downsizings" and the bleak future for college graduates in a "saturated market." There will always be change, change we like and change we don't like—but how prepared are we when it comes?

Take another close look at some of the major changes faced by ourselves, family members, friends and neighbors. Whatever the outcome, whether it involves great joy or tremendous sadness, each of these heavyweight events is at its very core about change.

marriage	death	aging
divorce	dying	moving
birth	grief	break-ups
dating	financial worries	make-ups
job loss	care giving	going back to school
promotions		

Many of us have gone through more than one of these major changes at the same time—truly a testament to our strength.

Divorce, marriage, childbirth and these others areas I've identified are among life's "change agents": like chemical agents used in high school science class, these are the "substances" that bring about change. In contrast to the instruments of change–the tools we use to modify our lives–these are the issues that lie beneath the changes.

Are any of the change agents mentioned here yours? No doubt something strikes a chord with you, either for yourself or for someone in your life. What tools are they using to get through a move, adjust to a new baby, or learn how to share custody of child with a former spouse?

Relationship Changes

*Nearly half of recent first marriages may end in divorce.**

I've included a statistic on divorce not because it's a new figure but because it shows that people continue to struggle with relationships and commitment, as they date and as they marry. Making your relationship a lasting one requires what I call a "relationship workout." And just like when you go to the gym to work off that extra ten pounds, it takes effort. In simplified terms, the same rules apply at the gym and in relationships: you get out what you put in.

A big part of seeing successful change means becoming a good communicator. This can be tough because we tend to think we're already letting our partners know what we want and how we feel. Communication also requires us to be great listeners, and we often fall short there too. We're "listening"—but not really hearing what the other person is telling us. That leaves both people frustrated.

---

* *Number, Timing, and Duration of Marriages and Divorces in 1996.* US Census Bureau, 2002.

Try this: repeat back in a couple of sentences what your girlfriend or boyfriend has just explained. In coaching this is called "validating." This process lets your partner know that you understand what's bothering him or her, and you're sensitive to it (whether you completely agree or not).

Here's an example. Lori has started the conversation and she's angry. This is not the first time they've argued about their relationship in recent weeks. If Kevin, her husband, wants to defuse the argument and open up a dialogue with Lori, the conversation might go something like this.

Lori: I really can't stand the fact that we spend so little time together. In order to make this marriage work it's going to take two of us. That's what you said, but I feel like you aren't doing anything to help. I know you have to keep two jobs—but I don't see you and the kids don't see you except for a few hours on the weekend. What are we supposed to do?

This time, instead of firing back with defensive statements, Kevin takes the time to confirm and understand what Lori has told him—to validate her feelings.

Kevin: Okay. I'm really trying to hear you out. Just give me a moment and listen to what I have to say too. So, what you're telling me is that I'm never home and I don't have time for the kids and you're really sick and tired of it at this point. I know you're frustrated and I know that almost all the burden is on you at home. But this time I want to see what we can both do differently with the time that we do have, at least until I can find a better job so I won't have to work two.

The technique of validating works wonders in changing the way people communicate. It can be used in many situations: when someone is upset and just wants you to listen, for example, or when a conversation is quickly turning into a full-blown argument. It's also something that we need to do more of when we're working out disagreements with bosses and co-workers.

Sometimes it's enough that the other person sees that we understand a few of their points. This common ground can transform an argument into a productive dialogue and create a platform for problem-solving.

Relationship Workout

Here are some other tips that I share with couples.

JENNIFER'S RELATIONSHIP WORKOUT

Know yourself first. Think about what you bring to the relationship so the two of you can discuss the value that each person brings.

Discuss your level of commitment at the appropriate time.

Appreciate your differences. Differences are what make you unique.

Encourage your partner to continue to explore some of the things they enjoy—their job, a hobby or some other activity.

Get to know more about your partner's interests so you can share in them if you'd like to.

Know when to take a "time out." It's a term we hear when children are misbehaving; here it means taking some time to think things through in the middle of a disagreement. Return to the discussion later when you can say what you really mean in a way that you won't regret.

Rekindle the romance. If you ever question whether you're being romantic, ask yourself: What would I do if this were our first or second date? If that date went well (and even if it didn't, despite your best efforts to impress), that's probably the way your partner would still like to be treated.

Change your tone and your talk! Change the way that you appreciate your partner. A note under a pillow or an unexpected compliment goes a long way.

Many of us are dealing with several relationship roles at one time. Think of a grandmother who is married, raising a grandchild and still working. Or a single mom who is dating a man with children of his own, or a woman in a dual-income family with her husband's children from a previous marriage. In all these cases, there is the "core" family and an extended family too. Whatever the family dynamics, dealing with so many types of relationships and responsibilities can be stressful.

Many women ask me how I deal with change effectively when it comes to my relationship, raising children and being successful at work. It's a very careful and delicate balance. And when it becomes unbalanced, the best repair has been my ability to laugh and then take a close look at what changes I can make to help things run a little more smoothly.

One key factor throughout has been my ability to adapt—to roll with the changes that are occurring at that moment. I actually got a little coaching in this area from my dad, though it wasn't until recently that I remembered this story. We were driving in the car when I was about 12 years old and somehow he and I ended up talking about life. You know how parents are. This sounds more mature than it actually was, but he was likely doing all the talking while I was sort of half listening.

While I can't remember the exact life lessons he gave me that day, I do remember him telling me to find a partner who was 'flexible.' I thought, "Hmm…. Then all that love stuff is probably overrated, if all I'm looking for is somebody who's 'flexible.'" I really had to think about that. My dad went on to say that "time goes on and the way you feel about a person is the same but different and better." By that point I was really confused. He did bring it down to my level, though, explaining that "you grow and change and so does he" (I imagine I didn't really have a handle on who "he" was).

Though my dad's advice hardly sounded romantic or sexy to a 12-year-old, as an adult I have to give him plenty of credit—flexibility goes a long way when your life is changing faster than you can blink. He also gave me a little precautionary advice about not expecting things always to stay the same. An oversimplified statement, perhaps, but definitely profound.

Many of us feel on top of the world when we first meet someone. We're absorbed in their every breath and we're convinced that we like everything about them. At this stage it can be easy to overlook certain things. So what if they leave their socks on the floor, and so what if they snore! Who cares! In the very, very early stages of romance you may find it adorable when they chime in and complete your sentences. Or even order your food.

But then, "something happens." Whether it's one year later or five years later, clients tell me that "what used to be so cute…isn't that cute anymore." I ask in return, "What has *changed*?" If he snored the day you met him and he's still snoring now—is he the one who has changed? Or has there been a change in what *you* like and what you find charming, desirable or even tolerable?

There is no wrong answer here; what's most important is that we fully explore the question. If a couple suddenly isn't getting along, the fundamental problem often has little to do with snoring, leaving underwear on the floor or bad table manners. These habits are annoying, yes, but not insurmountable—that is, if you still fundamentally like the person. The real issue is how we adjust to change.

Over time, we will experience changes in how we perceive things, how things affect us and how we react once we've determined a situation is more than we can stand. Going back to the thoughts of dear old dad: the idea of being flexible and adapting to change makes a lot of sense. Even though at our core we may still be very much the same as when we first met our partner, things are changing rapidly all around us.

When my husband and I first met I was a television intern home from college for spring break. He was already working as a manager for a major food company. Now fast-forward a couple of years into our relationship. We traveled all over the country, our parents were in good health, we had good jobs and life was splendid. Oops, here comes a major life change. Marriage. A move. A house. New jobs. Graduate school. A baby! Job losses and more new jobs. And that was all within the first two years of tying the knot. Talk about change…. What was I thinking?

Sometimes we do it to ourselves with the best of intentions, and other times it catches us off guard. We're not at all prepared for the change we're about to undergo. Better be flexible, I thought—a lot has happened since those first years of marriage.

When I rewind the mental "tape" of my life I marvel at the changes that have occurred within me and around me. My parents often tell me how much I've grown as a woman, a mother, a friend, a spouse. (But you

know how parents are!) Try rewinding the tape of your own life. Think about the changes—the relationships past and present, the jobs you've had. What can you take from those experiences to apply to your present and future? What did you learn that could be useful to the path you envision for yourself right now?

Acknowledging Your Changes

Here are some of the ways I have seen change turn into lasting growth in my life. I'm sharing this with you in the hope that it helps you to identify how you have grown, too—areas where you have already gone through change or are in the process of being enlightened. Use your *Life Changes Journal* to make a list of the changes you're seeing in yourself daily.

- The way I feel about the value of relationships, the quality of my relationships and my ability to communicate my emotions has changed tremendously.

- The way I value my time and my energy and the preservation of my body, mind and spirit has changed tremendously.

- My focus on achieving goals, and my feeling of what is important today versus what will be important a year from now, has changed tremendously.

- Making the time to have fun and enjoy my friends and family has become much more important to me.

- I have learned that even when a person 'knows me,' he or she doesn't automatically know exactly what I mean—especially if I don't say it.

- Taking ownership of my personal and professional gifts and knowledge, and sharing these gifts with others, has become much more significant to me.

- Taking that leap of faith to pursue my entrepreneurial vision was an act of great growth and change.

- I have made great progress in seeking to maintain loving intentions and thoughts even in the most difficult of circumstances.

- Refusing to let arguments, confusion or the negative thoughts of others consume me has been an area of positive change.

- I have learned to allow my spiritual self to rise to the surface and play a part in everything I do, with no apologies, fear or shame.

Your "life-changing sentences" are a metric that allows you to see how much you've grown. They also allow you to think about the areas in which you'd like to grow even more.

Chapter 4

Changing Your Life
One Step at a Time

"Becoming My Authentic Self"

*This letter is from Traci, who has a well-regarded career
in corporate communications. I had asked her a number
of questions about how change influenced her life.*

The hardest change I've had to deal with recently is having the
courage to be my authentic self in a relationship. While this may
sound like a natural way to "be," I was raised, like many women, to
please others. This can be a fake way of living—it is for me anyway. I
call this "doing pleasies." It's like when you don't want to do something
but feel guilty and do it anyway.

Well, my last relationship let me experience a new "gift" I gave to
myself. I had the courage to ask for what I needed, sometimes repeat-
edly, and the courage to leave when I realized his ambivalence toward
commitment and his desire to just live to work (without true passion)

would not change. This big change in myself has affected me in several ways. I now have a much clearer picture of who I am. I feel more worthy and empowered when it comes to my needs. I'm better able to communicate, and I'm more of a partner in a relationship. And most importantly, I now know that it's up to me to create my best life.

This also had an impact on me professionally. I am more direct when giving feedback—not as wishy-washy. I've become empowered to have my needs met in my career. It has also allowed me to see ways to create the career that is best for me.

This change was a decision I made. I can't remember when I put my imaginary "stake" in the ground, but I knew that I would not lose myself in another relationship. My transition was a process. I took tiny steps each day. Sometimes it would be a note I left for my boyfriend, other times it would be a conversation, but I would always make sure that my needs were included. Sometimes I would second-guess myself and need to remind myself that I *had* told him what I wanted—he'd just ignored it. I wasn't crazy—he was avoiding or minimizing me. I even raised a yellow flag, figuratively, and told him the "love boat" was sinking. He didn't see the "iceberg," and the ship sank. Finally I had had enough and the process was complete. With grace and love in my heart, I told him I couldn't continue our relationship because we needed and wanted different things.

After that experience, my best advice for handling change is: get clear, take steps, keep going and don't give up. Get help if you need it, and celebrate your courage. Everyone comes into your life for a reason, a season or a lifetime. Learn from everyone. The power of change means living life with passion and courage.

Traci, communications expert

Traci is a great example of how you can change your life a step at a time. When she faced setbacks, she saw them not as huge barriers but as learning experiences. If one technique didn't work, she continued to try new things. She did this in her relationship until she felt it was time to move on.

Traci uses the word 'courage,' which is very important. It takes exactly that to claim your life and let others know how you want to live it. Once we know this within ourselves then we can share it with others in our relationships.

Ask each other how you feel about commitment. What does that word mean to you, and how do you show it through your actions? What are the values that are most important to you in a relationship? And, yes, ask yourself and each other if you are flexible and willing to adapt when a significant change is underway.

Traci is correct when she points out that even the smallest steps eventually lead to huge strides. The goal is to keep moving forward. However, we can see from her letter and others that follow that taking those steps is difficult for many of us to do, especially when it comes to relationships. When change is on the horizon and people are contemplating divorce, separation or breaking up, there are often feelings of disappointment, pain, anger, anxiety, resentment and a whopping amount of guilt.

I bring up guilt because it seeps into so many scenarios in our lives. Many women who are newly divorced or in the process of getting divorced confide in me that their husbands were unfaithful on a number of occasions. Despite the infidelity, the women in these relationships feel an incredible amount of guilt. Some of them have explained in great detail how they tried to save their marriage by "changing" themselves rather than addressing the matter at hand—why the infidelity was happening in the first place. Some felt that if they were thinner or more attractive they might have a more committed relationship, one where their partner wouldn't look elsewhere for romantic escapades. However, this type of change does nothing to transform what is really at the 'heart of the matter.'

One of the first things I learned when I was getting my certification in professional coaching is that we make logical decisions and changes with our heads, but we make lasting changes and decisions with our hearts. Which types of changes are we more likely to be committed to and less likely to regret?

When you're faced with a decision that involves change, there's nothing wrong with asking yourself, "What should I do? What's the best plan for me?" That's making a logical and reasonable decision using your head. But I also urge my clients to use their hearts: we all have unique instincts to guide us during the difficult times in our lives. It's that idea of 'going with your gut feeling.' What is your inner voice telling you? If you aren't listening to this inner voice, think of a time when you were in an unexpected crisis and had to react quickly. What did that inner impulse tell you to do?

I tell people that my gut instincts have rarely led me down the wrong path. As long as my heart was in the right place, my head followed. When I was a reporter I would often rely on instinct to get my stories, especially when it came to breaking news. Still, I can't think of a more fitting example of going with your gut than when you become a caregiver to a sick or aging family member, or when a new baby is on the way. So many of us are members of the 'sandwich generation,' a group of people with an incredible amount of responsibility for both young children and aging parents. For many women, the time spent caring for younger and older family members represents a significant portion of their lives.

Dealing with change in your life is one thing; dealing with change when you don't have time to focus on your life is another. Women in particular tell me that they often don't get a chance to enjoy or fully digest a personal change because they're so busy doing things for others. This phenomenon cuts across marital status, race, income and other demographics.

Some young women tell me they are seriously considering opportunities that await them after college, but they're particularly concerned about how a change in *their* lives may affect others around them. Would it put a strain on their relationships if they decided to pursue graduate work or a career that took them far away? As we approach college age it is easy to fall into a game of 'follow the leader.' This is just as we are undergoing some of the most rapid changes in our lives—changes in maturity, responsibility and independence.

Into the Deep End: My Story of Overcoming Fear

Change is something we must face at every stage of our lives, from infancy on. The fears that we have as children often follow us well into adulthood. I remember that as a child I was afraid to swim. My dad was a great swimmer, while my mother barely dared touch a toe into the water. She had had a wonderful childhood, filled with all kinds of games and sports—but no one had ever nudged her to swim. She was a real bathing beauty with an hourglass figure. The downside to getting wet, as her friends affectionately said, was "you'll mess up your hair."

Well, her hair looked good but her swimming skills were lacking. My mother was determined not to pass this problem down to the next generation, so my parents enrolled me in swimming lessons at the YMCA in the heart of Chicago. The coach there was one of the top swimming coaches in the city. His philosophy for getting kids into the pool was not to let them work their way in gradually, but rather to have them jump off the diving board into the deep end—effectively breaking and shattering their fear.

Looking back, I believe I was fearful of the water in the first place because a few years earlier I might have drowned in a hotel pool had I not been saved by my dad. I remember going down deep into the water, feeling a rush of bubbles as I rose to the surface, coming up and gasping for a big breath of air and yelling "Get me outta here!"

Fortunately my dad was just a heartbeat way. Although I was fine, this incident was a change agent for me. It changed my level of comfort with water and my ability to have fun in it. So when I began those swimming lessons, I was extremely fearful of having to go into the deep end. This coach believed that if you wanted to conquer fear, your action would have to be swift. In a much more elementary way, I thought to myself, this is either going to be really, really good or really, really bad. I can remember changing my clothes and feeling the cold hard tiles under my feet. Swimsuit on, bathing cap ready, hit the shower. That's how the morning went. I was quietly nervous because I knew that a change was coming. Would this be a good change or a bad one?

Even when we're little—I was about seven at the time—we feel that overcoming a fear like this one is a positive change. But the hard part was actually doing it, actually embracing that belief and acting on it. Would this be the day that I actually climbed the steps to the diving board and walked to the end? Or would this be the day I took one look at that Olympic-size pool and ran away, never to return? After all, I didn't *have* to learn to swim. True, knowing how to swim would be safer and it made sense. But I could get by without it, and my parents would probably be okay if I never mastered this skill.

What was going through my mind at the time was, "Isn't it cruel for someone to take such measures—to make kids walk the plank and dive off into the ocean? I don't really need to change," I thought. "I don't need to be a swimmer!" But the funny thing about pushing past our fears and changing the things that hold us back is that we gain so much more than what we'd been afraid of—the dive, so to speak. We gain self-respect, courage and self-reliance. We gain wisdom and insight into the strength we have when we push ourselves to change.

So, if you're wondering what happened that day: I managed to creep up the board, roll my pudgy toes over the end and take a big deep breath. It really was a 'go for it' moment. I don't remember any kind of fancy dive, but I remember making a big splash and moving my legs as if I was running rather than swimming. I could hear the coach yelling my name and before I knew it I was up, gasping for air. I had done it—and I was still alive! I remember thinking, "I probably won't ever do this to *my* kids, but what the heck. I made it."

There was no better feeling in the world. My fear was broken and powerful changes had begun. It went far beyond the pool. The effects of the change carried over to school, camp, writing, school plays, singing and just about everything I did in those years. In fact, I'm convinced that the changes that were set in motion by that jump into the deep end carry over to this day. The courage and self-confidence that I discovered at age seven continue to help me in many valuable ways.

Now think about how you have broken through some of your own anxieties. As you write in your *Life Changes Journal*, ask yourself what fears are hovering around you now. How are they getting in the way of something important you'd like to accomplish? Writing down your thoughts will help you develop a plan to move past barriers that are holding you back.

Firing Up Financial Change

This is a good place to bring up a change agent that is a real "hot button" in many people's lives—finances. So many internal and external factors affect our relationship with money: whether we fear the subject or can talk about it easily, our values in regard to spending and saving, the areas of our lives that change when our financial status changes. And for many people, money is a measure of self worth.

Unfortunately, pegging your sense of personal value to your bank account can be dangerous, since financial status can change as quickly as the wind blows. This is especially true if you're spending more than you earn or living paycheck to paycheck without setting aside any savings. And as many of us know, concerns about changes in financial status–coupled with relationship worries and the tangible impact of a job loss–can drive even the most level-headed person over the edge. At the core of all the anxieties, of course, is change.

We learned earlier about the importance of being proactive and taking the lead—anything is possible when the potential for change exists. Many people are particularly sensitive to any fluctuation in their finances because they save very little and spend a lot. This common scenario in America leaves people on the edge when financial changes come to the forefront. Sometimes it's the loss of a spouse that affects one's finances (and we'll discuss the loss of our loved ones more later). Other times it's poor planning. We know that emergencies will come up–a leaky roof will need to be repaired or an old car will need to be replaced–but when the emergency happens we're often left scrambling. We had been operating on the assumption that a change *may*, rather than *will*, occur. When change strikes and it hits your wallet, are you prepared?

To explore this significant change agent you've got to explore yourself. Take a hard, honest look inside to see how you feel about money and the potential for change in your financial status. Imagine for a moment that you won the lottery—that's a change, right? What would you do with the money? I'm sure that many plans come to mind. A new home, a new car, or perhaps a luxurious vacation might be the first thing you'd splurge on. It all sounds great. But even for quite a few winners it's too good to be true. Some lottery winners still end up in debt. Were they ready for the change? Many were not, not when it came to following a plan to preserve a portion of those big winnings.

Often the money goes as quickly as it comes. But we needn't be lottery winners to see why preparing for financial change is so important. It's a matter of learning to expect the unexpected. It's not just smart—it helps to ease stress and allows us to take control of our lives.

I know the impact that external forces such as plant closings and layoffs can have. But sometimes our personal choices force change, too. Some of us want to change professions, or start a business, or fund our education while maintaining a full-time job. Others want to grow the dollars they have even when money is tight, and others are concerned about retirement and saving for college.

Think about the changes that you may have to make in order to bring your goals within reach. Here are some questions to get you started toward a financial plan that *you* control, regardless of the unexpected changes that may come your way. Think seriously about the questions and take some time to write your answers in your *Life Changes Journal*.

- What are my financial goals for the present and for ten years from now? List at least ten goals for each timeframe, starting with the most important ones.

- If I should experience a change in my financial status, will I be prepared?

- What are my "money values"? What types of things make sense for me to spend money on? Do I feel okay about using credit to pay for items I couldn't afford with cash?

- Do I make money only to spend it on things I enjoy, or do I grow it and invest for my future?

- How would I feel about myself if I lost my income?

- How much money do I have saved in the event I lose my job? How long could I get by without completely depleting my savings?

- What kind of insurance do I need and have? Mortgage, disability, life insurance?

- Do my partner and I agree on how to manage our money?

- Should I seek advice from a professional financial planner?

- How much money do I need?

- How much money do I want, and what would I do with it if I had it?

- As a parent, what messages am I sending to my kids about money?

- What can I do to educate myself about securing my financial future?

- What is my true financial status? What is my net worth? (This is the value of all the assets you own–car, house, investments, and so forth–minus the debt you owe–credit cards, car loans, student loans, etc.)

- How am I preparing for or currently sustaining my retirement years?

The way we feel about finances is extremely important. It is often said that sex, communication and money are among the biggest sources of stress for couples; I've certainly found money to be a top area that people want to improve upon in their work with a coach.

I recall having a cookout where my friends and I, along with our boyfriends and husbands, got into a heated debate about how our children (or babies to come) should spend money. It was interesting to see the adults revisit the experiences of their childhoods and link those times to how their own children should be raised. Two of the couples, including my husband and me, were divided–women on one side, men on the other–as to when our kids should have cars.

My husband had owned a car from a very young age. He grew up in southern Virginia and his dad had let him tinker on his first car and drive it around the yard from the time he was about 14. I, on the other hand, grew up in New Jersey, and learned to drive in a school parking lot. I practiced for weeks before taking my driving test. It was a very official process. I can remember my mom pulling out the old orange cones for

me to practice parallel parking. My brothers had gotten the same treatment before me.

What did this have to do with money? Regardless of our different introductions to driving, Joe and I had both wanted the same thing—a car. He remembers combining parts from three cars to get his first used Volkswagen Beetle ready for the road. I, on the other hand, had a new car—I often drove long distances for my summer jobs and my mother thought it would be safer.

The men at the cookout concluded that children should have what the women called a real 'hoopty.' You know, a car that screams, "I'm a college student!"—one like my husband's, which apparently had dents in the sides and a door falling off. The ladies, however, stuck to their guns and said that whatever it took, they'd rather spend the extra money to get their kids something they felt was safer.

As the conversation went on, very little was said about the cars our kids would actually drive someday. The focus was really on how we felt about our upbringings and the values we had surrounding money. I had gotten an allowance; Joe hadn't. If we were to give our own kids an allowance, what would be an appropriate amount?

Now, years later, our perspectives are completely different. The lines we drew in the sand back then are hard to see these days. It's all because of change. The children have grown—and we have grown and changed right along with them. Saving for college is the priority at center stage, not the question of a 'hoopty' versus a new car.

Hot-button issues like finances become so internalized that it's hard to separate the issue from our true selves. I ask you: do you drive the finances, or do the finances drive you? If you're in the driver's seat then you're better able to deal with unexpected bumps along the road. If you know what your financial goals are for this year then you can begin to modify the choices that are getting in the way of those goals. Would you like to save for a down payment on a house, or start contributing to your company's employee savings plan, or perhaps buy a vacation home or investment property? What changes will you have to make in order to move toward what you want or need?

Do you need to modify your spending habits?
Do you need to change your lifestyle?
Do you need to revise your goals?

These are all important questions, especially when the credit card bills are piling up. If we're going to take control of our finances, we need to know how to clean up our credit, and we need to change our habits of credit dependency.

Consumers spend billions of dollars on holiday purchases and shopping online. Great if you're receiving the gifts, but not so great if you're giving them and can't afford to. This spending comes with a hefty surcharge for the millions of Americans who are still paying for Christmas gifts the following June.

Now is the time to make sure your credit is in order. Whatever the season, there is good reason to get a copy of your credit report. A credit report gives you—and the companies that will potentially extend credit to you—specific information about your credit history, outstanding debt and the age of your accounts. For example, if a bank or mortgage lender is considering offering you a loan, they will want to know in advance whether you have a history of paying bills late and whether you've defaulted on loans in the past. All this information is there in black and white. The really good news, too, is that Americans are now entitled to receive a free credit report annually.

Here are a couple of ways you can receive your free report:

Go to www.annualcreditreport.com to access your annual credit report online for free.

Or call toll-free: 877-322-8228.

You can also complete the "Annual Credit Report Request" form, available on the Federal Trade Commission website (www.ftc.gov), and follow the instructions for sending it in by mail.

The three major commercial credit reporting bureaus are Equifax, Experian and TransUnion. When you order your credit report through one of them, you'll be charged a small fee but you'll also receive your credit score (see below.)

CONSUMER REPORTING AGENCIES

Equifax
1-800-685-1111
www.equifax.com

Experian
1-888-397-3742
www.experian.com

TransUnion
1-800-888-4213
www.transunion.com

If you have attempted to obtain credit in the past, you have a credit "score." Creditors use this figure in deciding whether or not to give you credit. The higher your score, the better off you are when it comes to borrowing money—it affects the interest rates you'll be offered on credit cards, mortgages and other loans. A better score gives you more options and keeps more money in your pocket by allowing you to borrow at a lower rate.

What if you went overboard and messed up your credit this holiday season—is there anything you can do about it? For starters, stop spending and focus on paying your bills. Purchase just the necessities as you seek to clean up your credit. It takes time, but here's how to get back on the right track:

Focus on paying bills on time.
Pay down outstanding balances.
Don't take on new debt.
Beware of scams that promise a quick post-holiday credit fix.

What will you have to change about your current lifestyle in order to make your financial dreams a reality? Have you written down and prioritized your goals? As a coach, I encourage you to modify your spending habits by limiting purchases to a certain amount each month. You're likely to embrace this change even more once you've taken control by devising a plan to save money or eliminate debt.

What changes need to take place *inside* you? Internal change is far greater than external change: it's the difference between being told to do something and pursuing it on your own. This, again, is the 'buy-in,' and this is where change gets exciting. When you have committed to a change you can feel its progress within and around you—and you'll find yourself more inspired than ever.

Chapter 5

Your Internal Power Fuels Change

When we realize our internal power, it is fierce. That is why I believe this chapter in particular can be life-changing. I was inspired to write this section because I sincerely believe in the great strength and capabilities we have within us. When I pray and worship, I am restored. But that alone is not the end of the story—nor should it be.

We're often taught to see ourselves as physical structures made up of muscle tissue and bones, like the plastic skeleton in an anatomy class. It's all a very sterile process when we go for a physical or get treated for a cold. But the beauty of the body is that it, too, changes and adapts. It boosts our adrenaline when we need that rush of energy to get out of harm's way, or for more ordinary needs like performing well in a meeting after putting in a 12-hour day. The body repairs damaged skin and muscle, and can even adjust to compensate for the loss of an organ.

As a woman, I feel that the most amazing experience was the change my body went through as it prepared for childbirth and the miracle of breastfeeding my babies. It's incredible to think that we can grow a complete human being inside us until the moment when the body knows it's time to deliver. How much the body knows, and how little we do to appreciate its transformations. These miracles of the body show us just how powerful we are.

With these remarkable capabilities in mind, think of the power that *you* have through your body. We are as capable as the bodies that God gave us—but we often fail to acknowledge the miracle that lies within. Knowing that our bodies are masters of the art of adaptation under the most challenging circumstances, how can we not appreciate our power to make tremendous life changes?

Intuition, Instincts and Your Inner Voice

Feel the power that you have within and think about the changes that you're preparing to make, knowing that your body is there to help you. Combine the body's abilities with the healing power of the mind and you've got an incredible combination. You've heard the saying "Mind over matter." When it comes to change this proverb speaks volumes. As you contemplate the changes you're facing, think about using your body and your brain together to solve a problem or achieve a particular goal. Use the triple I's:

Use your *intuition*.
Use your *instincts*.
Use your *inner voice*.

Imagine the rapid beat of your heart when you feel anxious or when you're in the midst of an unpredictable situation. Oftentimes at these moments you have no alternative but to rely on your intuition, instincts and inner voice. These are gifts that all of us are born with. Intuition is the "sixth sense." We use our instincts in combination with concrete knowledge about our surroundings. When you smell smoke, your instincts tell you that a fire is near. Your inner voice is extremely important too, but how well it works is really up to you. Do you acknowledge your inner voice? Do you know when it's speaking to you and understand its message?

Suppose you were doing some research about starting a small business. You've been smart in doing all the things that will help you determine whether the time is right for this change in your life. You've put together a business plan; you've looked carefully at how this move could affect your finances, your time and your lifestyle. Now, once you've gathered all the information you can, sit quietly and allow your inner voice to speak. What is it telling you?

Listening to this voice may turn out to be the most important part of your decision-making process: balancing the facts with guidance from our inner voice prepares us to live with the outcome of our decisions. Whether the business takes off like a rocket or struggles and ends up closing its doors, when we use the power of that inner voice there are few regrets. Moms use it, Fortune 500 executives use it, doctors use it. When these experts realize after careful analysis that the question facing them isn't a black-and-white matter, they have to ask themselves—What do I do?

As the expert in your own life, you, too, should look inside for guidance. Allow your inner voice to help you weigh your options after you've looked at the facts. That voice is what our grandparents and great-grandparents used to raise children, to leave their homelands and travel to faraway places. They didn't have the Internet, of course, and many of them didn't have the technology that was considered sophisticated in their day. They used their intuition, instincts and inner voice to provide food for their families and to care for them when they were sick.

Changing Family Dynamics

Change can be difficult and complex, but if we look inside ourselves, we'll find everything we need to manage it successfully. In an earlier chapter I discussed change agents that are familiar to many of us, like job loss and divorce. I have a story that echoes the power of change so strongly that I must share it with you. This one involves relationships, and the power of change when it comes to weddings and the blending of two families.

I hadn't been paying attention to my own inner voice with regard to this topic until it finally dawned on me that there was a message here.

Over the past year, about half a dozen women I know have told me about their children getting married. All of these women were friendly acquaintances, people I'd met at the gym or at a party or two. So—Great, I'd say when they shared the news, congratulations; tell me more about what's planned. But to be honest, if I'm sweating and panting and looking at my minutes on the treadmill, I'd really love to hear more about it when I can at least dry off and smell a bit more fragrant! Still, I'm a sucker for a good conversation, and as time went on I realized that I needed to listen to my inner voice.

Clearly there was a message here that was not really about weddings but about the power of change. So there I was, sweating and running and walking and doing all I could to keep up with the treadmill, and more and more I was engaged in conversations about wedding plans and developments within the families—some of which were positive and others not so positive. And there I was at parties, with the people around me talking about their children who had recently married. Hmm, I thought. Is it me or is there a common theme here? Of course, timing plays a part in this, but like so many discoveries in my life, this story was presenting itself in a powerful way and needed to be examined. Each new personal story I heard brought something new into my view.

I met one of these women while I was on vacation. She explained to me that her son was getting married and she saw her own relationship with him going down the tubes—"slipping away," as she phrased it. "He didn't even send me a card for Mother's Day this year," she said, "and I barely got a phone call." She went on to tell me that both she and her husband found the girlfriend and her family "cold." In the mother's opinion, the couple spent little time with her and *her* family, and they were making purchases—a car, a new house—that they simply couldn't afford. "He's doing this just because *she* wants it," she said.

Now, switch gears with me for a moment. Here's where the next mother of a groom enters the picture. In this woman's situation, as she explained it to me, a very proper New England couple had raised a lovely daughter and a lovely family, and now they were coming together with her own large Italian family. Although the families were different, she said, "It's a match made in heaven." Smiling, she went on to make glowing comments about the young lady and her relatives. "They came down for the holidays," she said, "although my son does spend a lot of time with her family." She added, "They really do want me involved in the wedding plans."

And for another twist, enter mom number three. We met at a party and started talking when we discovered that we both had sons, though hers were adults with their own families. The sons were close in age and had all married recently, within a year of each other. This mother had undergone some big life changes—and she was now a new grandmother, too.

This woman was generous with compliments for her grandchildren and her sons, but had little to say about their new brides and their families. This certainly wasn't a coaching session–it was simply a passing conversation–but I was curious as to why this was the case. I didn't pry, but by concentrating on listening rather than talking (which I am truly a fan of), I was able to see exactly where the conversation was headed. Over the shrimp cocktail she blurted out to me, "Do you know that none of my daughters-in-law know what to call me?" "What do you mean?" I asked. She replied: "Since they don't know what to call me, they don't call me anything!"

It was only natural for me at that point to throw in a coaching question. "How does that make you feel?" "I really don't like it," she said. "They won't ever say 'Mrs.' or 'mom' or anything like that. Only—one of them has said to me recently, I don't know what to call you—is it okay if I call you 'mom?'" "And how does that feel?" I asked. "Now, *that* I love," she said.

There is a strong common thread in what these three mothers are experiencing: change, of course. It's not just about getting married. It's not just about what you wore or how much you were or were not involved in this huge day in a family's life. The son's life is changing, his bride's life is changing, and each of the families is encountering tremendous changes as well.

Now, before we dig deeper into family relationships and change, let's bring in mom number four. She and I met at a social event where I had brought my own mother. Like my mom, this woman had boys and grandchildren. The two mothers met and started talking, and before long they were sharing information about their families. When I joined the conversation I found her particularly interesting and quite refreshing. Again, I did a lot of listening. I was especially fascinated by her story about how she and her husband had been elementary school sweethearts.

She had known the young man who would one day be her husband since her early childhood; when she was about thirteen even her mother had said they were something special. The calmness in her voice, and her obvious joy at being together for so long–from their early friendship, to his time away in the military, to their marriage soon after–reminded me of something out of a romance novel.

As she talked about the changes they'd gone through over the years, one aspect of her story struck me in particular: I got a strong sense that her family was able to stay connected and unified, yet each individual was also able to maintain their independence. My ears perked up when she said that her two sons had followed her and her husband to the South when they retired. She went on to say that she couldn't be happier for the whole family, because her daughters-in-law brought them all so much joy.

Realizing that she was the fourth mom within a very short period to talk to me about children, marriage and in-laws, I thought to myself, what's the difference here? This time I had to ask: "How have you cultivated this relationship with your sons' wives?" She said, "I really didn't. It started when the boys were little—long before they were married." She explained that she had always been very close to her sons. As they got older, she had encouraged them to see the value of the relationships she and her husband had with their own in-laws. The sons had learned through watching these role models that a wife didn't have to compete with her mother-in-law. "I give them space and I love them both," she said.

The sons helped carry on the positive relationships by talking with their future wives about how significant the family was to them. "People always assume that boys are going to leave home and never come back again," she said. "If your family is important to you, it doesn't have to be that way."

Does this story sound too good to be true? It's true nonetheless. When the parents left the northeast, they didn't expect their adult children to follow, but they welcomed them when they did. They gave them space to make their own mistakes but also offered a safety net of love and support. And in the midst of these changes–moving to a different part of the country, leaving their jobs and saying goodbye to family and friends–the parents kept the focus on themselves and let the lives of their adult children and extended family continue to evolve around them. The mother joked that she moved south only to end up living down the street from one of her sons and close to the other one as well.

So, four different families and four different ways of handling changing relationships. Change that brings new people into a family unit can be very difficult to adjust to. It takes considerable time to digest: the union of the couples has a tremendous impact on the people close to them.

Does that mean that the new couple shouldn't be the focus of the family as the big day approaches, or shouldn't make decisions on their own as they plan their all-important nuptials? No. Excitement, stress and anxiety are all natural feelings when families are coming together for the first time. The key is that if families plan to co-exist with their "new" families, they're going to have to work at making the changes work for them. The moms will have to adapt along with the dads and sons and daughters.

All of these mothers had husbands who were sons too, and were now sons-in-law. But this was different. Now they would have to learn what it meant to work with another family that had its own traditions. As I listened to the mothers' stories, I thought about how much they missed spending time with their sons. How would they all share each other's time when, as many of us say, we have so little time to share? On the surface, each of the individuals involved in planning these weddings had a handle on the details of the day. But the change that accompanied the unions would have profound effects for everyone in the inner circle.

Many of us fear that changes such as these mean losing a special relationship with a loved one. I heard one of the moms say, "It's just not going to be the same." Well, of course it's not going to be the same. The families and friends of these newlyweds were going to see their lives changing rapidly. Friends would see a couple evolving as they took on new commitments and responsibilities. Accepting these changes as a natural part of life would *help* their friendships; deciding that change would cause their relationships to dissolve could only have negative effects. The families would have to allow their sons and daughters to grow in ways they'd never seen before—and couldn't control. Some of us believe that if we can stop things from changing, we have absolute control over our lives and can dictate change to others. This kind of thinking is a very slippery slope. Evolving along with the changes beyond our control and

implementing changes that improve our lives is the way to go—especially when it comes to the relationships we value the most.

"The Empty Nest"

Jamie, also a mother, writes a poignant letter about big changes she experienced concerning her two college-age sons.

Between Thanksgiving and Christmas of 2003, I had major surgery that I was not prepared for emotionally, but physically I was ready for the relief it would bring. My emotions swung from one extreme to the other, but eventually I got my emotions under control. It actually took about a year following the surgery to really begin to feel good about myself. During this same time, my home life was in transition. My sons had gone away to college and I had to deal with the emotions that go with this life-changing event.

My life had revolved around the boys. Every move I made was a coordinated effort to ensure that they were where they needed to be and I was at whatever meeting I needed to be at. This had been my life for about nineteen years.

One son was attending college out of state and the other was about three hours from home. Sure, I knew that they would be leaving, and I had planned to be ready. But time got by me and it turned out that I was *not* ready. There were people around me who knew how close I was with my sons and knew that I was not going to do well, but I assured them that I would be fine. Fine, I told them, because I always knew they would be leaving. That was so far from the reality of the first day of them gone. My home was the quietest it had ever been. I longed to hear their music playing and to see them walking around with their cell phones attached to the side of their faces.

Fortunately, my sons called on my first day without them and they began to encourage me. I was the parent, yet they were saying, "Pursue your dreams," like I had always said to them. They knew that I had always wanted to take a Bible course and that was the first thing they told me to do. As they said, "You've got more than enough time now."

It took another couple of months for me to begin to research and find a place that offered what I wanted to pursue. After finding the place and registering for the course, it hit me that I was really getting ready to do something for me. I was actually going somewhere alone and knew no one there. This was so not me, and I really thought about not attending. I had never gone anywhere, other than work, where I did not know someone or go with someone I knew. Needless to say, this has been the best thing I've done. I have met with wonderful people who have become great sources of enjoyment. Taking the Bible course and wanting to make some advances in my job has led to me taking more courses. My plans are just to take courses that interest me.

So, to sum up, in dealing with the aftermath of surgery and the emotional changes of being in the empty-nest stage, I have been able to develop a confidence in myself. Now, I can go places alone and take classes and do well. It may not seem like a lot, but for an introvert like me, this has been a great accomplishment.

Jamie, historical records specialist

The beauty of this letter is its simplicity and sincerity. Jamie was going through one of the biggest changes of her life—learning to let go while continuing to love and guide her children when needed. At the same time, she was learning to love, guide and nurture herself. She longed to hear the music and voices that children bring into the home, but their vitality could not be a replacement for the life that we need to have within ourselves. When the house grows quiet, that is a time not to retreat into ourselves but to focus on our inner restoration and rejuvenation.

As we share real-life stories about the empty nest (and this also applies to caring for others who didn't live with us), it is important to recognize that this is a stage of powerful transition. Jamie had to change her thinking and her way of living. Her schedule would be different and would allow her to do more things for herself. She recognized that she would need the support of her children and others to help her weather these changes. You can see how Jamie evolved and grew throughout this powerful change in her life and how valuable it was for her to go through the process.

Let's revisit the phases of change I explained earlier.

Phase I–Universal Motion
Phase II–Positive or Negative Response
Phase III–Enlightenment and Discovery
Phase IV–Voluntary or Involuntary Change
Phase V–Transition
Phase VI–Transformation

Universal motion is the energy that surrounds and evolves around us. In the stories we've just looked at, much of that energy was focused on changes in parenting and roles within the families. Many types of transition were taking place in these women's lives: the transition from loving mother to loving grandmother or mother-in-law, or from the mom who sees you every day to the mom who sees you off to college; and for one of the mothers in this chapter, there was the transition from worker to retiree.

Jamie experienced sadness and anxiety in having to face surgery and send her children off to school at the same time. But her positive outlook was vital to her ability to cope with this situation and grow from it. In Phase IV, she knew it was time for a voluntary change. She became enlightened when her children convinced her to take the Bible classes. The very same children she had raised, instilling in them the importance of moving forward, were now the voices of reason in her life. In essence, they were giving back to her what she had given them—the message that change is progress, even when it means being separated from your loved ones.

Now, you can see how Phases V and VI are coming into shape. During her transition phase, Jamie was testing the waters to see how she would handle doing things on her own. She was being tested–her own personal test of sorts–to see whether she would be true to herself and follow through with the course she wanted to pursue. Would she use this newfound energy to her advantage? Since we know the ending to the story, we know that the answer is yes! The ability to move beyond her belief that she couldn't achieve things by herself, or do things that weren't focused squarely on the children, was a major victory for her self-esteem.

Welcome Phase VI: Jamie's transformation. I was so excited for Jamie because she is a great example of how tough changes can allow us to triumph over the things we're afraid to face. She transformed into a confident woman on the inside and out—one who was no longer afraid of taking on new challenges. And most significantly, she was learning to put herself first at a period in her life when she had the time to do it. She was ready to nourish her mind, body and soul with religious courses that would feed her spirit while she also welcomed new challenges at work.

What lessons do I want you to take away from this chapter? At the beginning I explained my belief that there is incredible strength and capability to be found within ourselves. No matter how challenging the change I'm facing, I am restored when I pray and worship. How are you restored as you prepare for change? Let's go through some thought-provoking questions together. Take some time to write your answers in your *Life Changes Journal*. Again, read the questions and allow yourself to think seriously about how you will take ownership of the changes you want in your life.

- What unique qualities do you possess that show your strengths in times of change?

- What are some of the ways that you can put yourself first in the face of change, even when you're feeling overwhelmed?

- Where are the sources of support in your life that will help you evolve successfully through change—perhaps a family member, friends or a mentor?

- Think about the space in your life that opens up to new opportunities when you learn to let go. What can you let go of to provide for a new opportunity as a significant change is underway?

Power Plays and Tapping Into Positive Change

Let's look at some of the ways that you can tap into your personal power for positive change. I call these "power plays."

> A power play can be something very calculated and obvious in the way it changes your life. It can also be an act or decision that seemed insignificant at the time, but as you explore it you begin to see its greater importance.

As an example, let's look at a power play that pertains to your health—specifically, losing weight. How many diets have we all tried? Ten, maybe twenty over the years? When I ask a group of people what they're going to change or do differently this time around, many enthusiastically say, "I'm going on a diet, one that really works!" But is it the diets that fail us, or are we failing to change our old habits? For so many of us, even after losing weight we gain it back quickly. We think of the diet as a quick repair job rather than a long-term improvement in our lifestyle.

With so many of us still struggling to lose weight, finding a power play that works is truly life-changing. Perhaps it's time to rethink our strategies when it comes to diet and exercise. Lasting power plays start out with small, attainable goals—goals that help you retrain yourself for long-term change. Think of changes that can be made beyond the diet itself. What are some other power plays that you can put into practice, in either large or small ways? Talk to your doctor about changes in your lifestyle that can make your weight loss plan more effective, such as:

eating healthy snacks
packing your lunch the night before work or school
taking the stairs
walking 20 minutes a day
drinking water to keep hydrated
watching your portion sizes
having an annual physical

Now think about the benefits of weight loss and fitness that go beyond dieting and lead to lasting life changes:

improving overall health
boosting self-confidence
raising energy levels
potentially increasing life span
staving off certain diseases

As we look at our lives and think about improving them, I encourage you to change your attitude and your approach. How we feel about ourselves and our bodies can lead us on a crazy quest for perfection. Health and happiness in our lives grow from the inside out. I want you to have the healthiest heart, the clearest head and the strongest bones you can have. Saying it is not enough. With obesity rates rising, we have to be realistic if we want to stave off disease and sustain our lives—by radically changing our lifestyles to include healthy eating and exercise.

Think about what has prevented you from making a change that lasts. The good news is that for many of us, we have the desire to be healthy but we lose momentum. We need some encouragement to keep us going, which is not a bad thing. Use your journal to write down your health habits each week. When you use your journal to record the foods you're eating and the amount of exercise you're getting, you can quickly see which actions are supporting your healthy life changes and which ones are not.

The idea is that you aren't just dieting—you're taking a new approach to changing your health for the better, forever. As someone who has struggled with her weight since early childhood, I know it is never too late to begin again. Each day is a chance to change. Remember that if you get off track, you can pick up tomorrow and begin again.

Power Play Questions

What power do I have to change my life?

How have I used my personal power for positive change in the past?

What am I seeking to change in my life right now?

Why are these changes important to me?

How committed am I to making these changes happen?

What is my deadline for accomplishing these changes?

What are three things I can do to keep focused on my goals?

What changes are happening around me or to me that are involuntary?

How can I use power plays right now, as part of either voluntary or involuntary change?

What will these specific power plays be?

Chapter 6

Managing Change Effectively

As much as change can revolutionize and reinvigorate our lives, it can also come with a tremendous amount of fear. Many of us see the changes in our lives as a burden that forces us to learn or do something new. We'll look more closely at life changes and loss, and the strength we have even during the most difficult of times.

"Learning to Let Go"

*Erika writes about a profound personal experience and
the challenge of accepting one of the biggest changes in our lives.*

As I was growing up, there was one constant and she stood all of five feet tall. She was a dynamo that wouldn't or couldn't be stopped. We were what many considered underprivileged. This, surprisingly, was a fact I never knew until they told me in school. My mother made sure we were comfortable, and if we wanted for anything, we did not miss it. She worked every day. She cleaned others' homes, and came back to make sure hers was taken care of. She had four young girls who she protected with the fierceness of a lioness in the jungle. She made sure that we knew what it meant to work for what we got. She had two favorite sayings: "If it's worth having, it's worth working for," and "If you're good at what you do, you don't have to hard-sell it." My most vivid memories are of her working in the kitchen, with Motown on her record player and her singing in the background, or her standing over the ironing board watching her soap operas or *Perry Mason* or even *Gunsmoke* on TV. But the constant factor here was that she was working, moving all the time.

Even after we all grew up and went our merry ways, she was still there, involved. When I finished college and moved 90 miles away to Washington, DC, she came to visit me in my first apartment. I was so proud of that place. It was spacious and was in a nice complex. I couldn't afford much so I bought used furniture and made my own drapes and covers for the sofa and chair. I had cleaned especially for her visit. I shopped to fill up the refrigerator. I went all out to impress on her how well I was doing. She came in, smiled, looked around and said very little. The next day, I went off to work and came home. I smelled the food before I got to the door. I knew she would be busy, but I had no idea just how busy. I opened my door and looked around. The little dynamo had not only prepared dinner, she had completely rearranged every item of furniture in my apartment. I walked in, shocked. I couldn't believe it. What made me really upset was not the fact that she had rearranged everything—I knew I could just put it all back. What upset me was that now it was all perfect and I didn't want to put it back!

A few years later, she started having trouble with her legs. They just didn't seem to be dependable anymore. They even began to give out on her when she walked up stairs. Finally, after a few years of testing and false solutions, the diagnosis came in. My mother had multiple sclerosis. She couldn't depend on her legs or her hands anymore. She had taken up crocheting and every one of us had vividly colored blankets for our beds and our kids' beds and any other miscellaneous spaces that needed covering. Now, though, the things that she used to make look so easy seemed to take twice as long. We eventually had to get a wheelchair for her.

Then one Thanksgiving, my mother was sitting at the table and we were preparing dinner for our annual family get-together. I looked at this person kneading the bread, and I did not recognize the woman who used to run you down, grab you by whatever she could get a hold of, and dispense whatever judgment was required for one of her energetic daughters. She had gotten old before her time and she looked sick. The strength was there, but only in her eyes and in her heart.

Life brings about all manner of change. You grow, you shrink; you make mistakes, sometimes you learn from them, sometimes you don't; you grow-up, you get old…but there are some images that you, reasonably or unreasonably, hold sacred. I preach to my kids that you have to be flexible and prepare for changes, that you can't let the unexpected send you into a big and unrecoverable tailspin. I tell them that you allow yourself some emotional, even hysterical, reaction time. Then you sit back, cut it out, say "Enough of that" and move forward. But still, some changes are just too hard to accept. My little dynamo died about 10 years ago. She was wheelchair-bound, but she could still take care of herself. She caught a cold because the maintenance people in her apartment would not properly adjust the heat and she developed pneumonia.

Change. No more sage advice. No more direct and very honest opinions. No more meddling into family matters, no more free and unsolicited advice, no more coming around and rearranging my life and making everything all better. Change—you're supposed to expect it and accept it, but some changes are just too hard to get used to.

Erika, computer design expert

My sincerest thanks go out to Erika for sharing this letter. You can feel the tug and the battle that Erika is still going through, ten years after her beloved mother's passing. She is not alone. As I was writing this book it occurred to me that this was a year in which I had gone to several funerals—more than I'd ever gone to in such a short amount of time. I was uneasy and searching, as Erika describes, for a way to deal with this pain and sadness.

I believe these feelings were so pronounced for me because my own parents were having health problems at the time. My mother had recently had a stroke, which led to the lowest emotional point in my life. I felt uncertainty and fear. Things were definitely changing. And the timing of these events was uncanny: the day of my mother's stroke, another friend lost his mother to cancer. All year long we seemed to hold our breath as we waited to see what would happen next. I turned to my coaching circle and to my friends and family. The fear of losing my mother was engulfing me with each and every breath. I couldn't sleep and I couldn't eat. I was struggling to accept the fact that a big change was underway. Like Erika, I grew up with that "dynamo" for a mom too. The kind of mom who tells it like it is, but has a heart so big it couldn't be measured. As time went on and uncertainty over her condition lingered, my thoughts grew darker and my heart heavier. How would I go on? How could I be the cornerstone of support for others when my own heart was breaking?

I didn't ask God to change the situation. What I did ask for, night after night, was the perseverance, strength and clarity to deal with the situation and do all I could to help. I prayed with such intensity that God would help me to change my perspective. There was no doubt that I wanted my mother to be well and to be free of pain and anguish. But I prayed a very careful and focused prayer—one that would allow me to bring about change in my life when I was not in control of the situation. I knew that I needed to be a solider and not sit on the sidelines, debilitated by my fears. I knew that I needed to see light rather than darkness if I was going to help myself or anyone else. I needed to change my thinking.

As we've seen in the personal stories throughout this book, change is working all around us, at all times. What happened next is a testament to that process. One day while I was driving, I had an epiphany. I literally felt that a weight had been lifted from me. My mind was suddenly cleared of the stresses that had made it feel like it was going to explode. The knot in my stomach was gone and my heart was no longer heavy.

All of this was the result of a single thought popping into my head: no matter what happens in life, we are all "on loan." Perhaps it came from all those years covering financial news on television—but the thought was divine. It felt wonderful and released me of the sinking worries that I had about my mother's fragile health. The concerns were still there, yes, but not the overwhelming anxiety. How could this be? As I kept driving, I thought hard about this revelation. I knew why it had been sent to me and I was deeply thankful. I had prayed for clarity and strength; now I needed to know more. What does it mean that we're "on loan"?

I continued to let my thoughts flow. If we're on loan, I said to myself, that means that life on this earth—on the earthly side—is merely temporary. This is what really got me. In this internal dialogue between myself and God, he was telling me that time is short and it is not guaranteed. A very sad thought, perhaps, if you don't change your thinking. But this was about change and seeing things differently. Now that I understand that we're on loan, I thought to myself, how do I want to spend the time that I have right now? I realized how eternally grateful I was for the time that I'd had already with my mother and father and family and friends.

If we are God's, then there is a time when he calls us, and our time on this side of our existence comes due. Our life here is a temporary situation—and if we realize that and cherish it, we will change the way we think, share, love and value one another. I thought, I'd better get my butt in gear and live in this moment. I need to treasure what I have and not long for things that may or may not come to pass. Out of an extremely difficult experience came an incredible life change. That epiphany inspired me to write this book, and made me want to show others how change, no matter how challenging, can provide us with insights that will carry us through difficult times for the rest of our lives.

My Journey: Letting Go, Bit by Bit

You've probably heard the saying, "Time brings about a change." It's one of those sayings my mom used when my brothers and I were growing up. I didn't quite know what it meant back then. My mother's family was from the islands and had many sayings, so you just didn't ask why a bird in the hand was better than two in the bush when it came time to do homework. What the heck did that have to do with history and science or anything else? Now, of course, I get it. Completing homework for both those subjects tonight was the sensible thing to do—just in case you should wake up tomorrow and find your book missing!

The saying "Time brings about a change," however, is one my mom used when she reflected on how different someone or something had become. If you fast-forward to my adult years, her words could apply to a very rapid and notable change that my family went through when my older son was in high school. He had been accepted into a national scholars' program held at Princeton University the summer after his freshman year. For a big part of that summer he would eat on campus, sleep on campus and attend classes for about seven hours a day. This change would be a test of my ability to let go.

The program was a rigorous one with very high expectations for its students. It also offered them a lot of independence. There was just one problem: I wasn't ready to let go. And what's more, this weepy feeling was like a virus that spread quickly through the house—no one else was prepared to have him leave either. It's a funny thing, though. Change has a way of letting us know in advance that it's coming. It's just a matter of whether we're paying attention or not.

Weeks before he was scheduled to leave, I remember thinking that I'd finally arrived at the point where I could officially say I had a teenager. I determined this milestone not by his age or size but by the number of minutes he used on his cell phone. All of a sudden, a massive number of calls were coming in and going out; instant messages were coming in and rolling out quickly too. The beauty of this situation was that as I started to look closely at why I was behaving the way I was, I realized that yes, he was growing up—but I was growing too.

I was being asked to reexamine my views on control and boundaries and trust in the parenting process. I had been rushing to set new rules and define new parameters. Then one night my husband said to me, "You were a teenager once, right?" Still—this was different. This time I was the mom and he was *my* son and changes were happening rapidly. I can remember feeling like I was losing control as each phone call came in. But in reality I wasn't out of control. I was afraid and I made change the culprit. I asked myself over and over again, Will he be okay? Will he be safe?

The problem at that moment was that I wasn't using my three I's— my instincts, intuition and inner voice. In truth, a change was underway that was going to affect our family dynamics. We would feel it deeply even though it would be temporary. It was a glimpse of what was to come. It was the beginning of letting go, bit by bit.

I was resistant to the changes around me as my son was doing what only came naturally—growing, exploring, trying new things. This would be the first of many changes as it sank in that there was officially a teenager in the house. It all took my emotions and actions to a new level. I was very proud but at the same time anxious: what would it be like to be separated from someone I'd seen just about every night of his life? And after we'd gone through so much to adjust to his absence, what would it be like when he returned at the end of the program? Who would have changed more—him or us?

At first the answer to this question in my mind was, Well, him of course. Obviously he would have changed more, after seeing and doing things for the first time and meeting so many new people. In so many ways, he was being nudged to adapt to a new level of independence. But now I think we were tied—he grew an incredible amount and so did I. It was a big step for me to stand aside and allow the process to happen, and to accept that allowing him to make his own decisions might mean allowing him to make his own mistakes.

Yes, tremendous change will happen—and fast. Whether we are fifteen years old or fifty, when we allow for changes like these we stretch ourselves. But what grows out of it is a collection of experiences that gives us a more worldly perspective. We might not know what we're capable of until we are nudged to try something different.

It's like getting lost. It's uncharted waters for us. Do you dread getting lost like most of us do? I used to. When we're lost it's unfamiliar and even a bit scary. I believe this is so uncomfortable for us because it makes us feel vulnerable. We're not in control, and we don't know how long the situation will last or whether we'll see our way through it.

I had never sent a son off to college before, so there was a feeling of losing control. But I had to change my thinking. By limiting myself to seeing only one perspective–one that included negative feelings or doubt–I would also limit the wonderful joy and happiness there was to receive in the midst of this incredible accomplishment.

A new opportunity for one son meant a different kind of opportunity for the other. While my older son had been an "only" child for seven years before his little brother was born, now the tables would turn. I started out feeling lost, but when I changed my thinking I realized I was very lucky. I would now have a chance to deepen my bond with my younger son by spending one-on-one time with him like we had never done before. We essentially became a tag team. Where I went, he went too. We went to the movies together, played basketball together (at that point he was desperate) and ate our snacks together. Whatever there was to do, we did it together.

Many of us experience a sense of urgency when we feel like we can't find our way. I want you to see how getting lost helps us to find a new route or discover something unexpected. When we change our perspective we no longer have to feel lost. Instead, feel lucky.

Chapter 7

The Metamorphosis–
Change and the Fear
of Getting Older

*Metamorphosis: a marked change in
appearance, character, condition, or function.**

Congratulations. By reading the first six chapters of *Life Changes* you've learned about many aspects of the power of positive change, including learning to let go, listening to your inner voice and overcoming fear. In this chapter you'll embark on another essential part of your journey: addressing the aging process and the fear of getting older.

Aging is arguably the biggest change in our lives. It's certainly a challenge for many of us as we're bombarded by the media with impossibly youthful images. The bottom line is that many try to escape the reality of aging, while comparatively few embrace it. But realizing the power of aging can change your life. I found it important to write about this because I often hear coaching clients impose limits on themselves and what they're capable of accomplishing because of their age.

---

* *The American Heritage College Dictionary.*

"Middle Age to Senior Age"

*Judy, a school nurse, talks about how time and the aging process
were no match for her mother's incredible strength and strong will.*

Aging and the progression of life can be an amazing but difficult
process. I have watched the changes in my mother's life over the past
fifteen years. My mother experienced the deaths of her siblings, husband and then her own declining health. The process of watching a
parent progress from being a healthy, energetic woman to an older
person fighting to keep her dignity while being ill and in pain is very
difficult.

She was always a strong and stoic person. She never exhibited fear
or anxiousness during my childhood or young adulthood. My mother
became the last surviving child of five siblings. She is the third child
in the order of birth. She was able to overcome the death of her old-
est and youngest sisters. These two sisters died within twelve hours of
each other. My mother was responsible for guiding the family through
planning and executing the funeral and burial arrangements for both
of these sisters. She was unbelievably strong.

Her younger and only brother died five years later. She assisted
her sister-in-law in caring for her brother for many years and when he
passed, she was very involved in assisting the family in dealing with his
death. My father, her husband, died three years after her brother. My
mother was again extremely strong. She nursed my father through two
and a half years of illness from recurring strokes prior to his death. She
dealt with his death with great dignity. My mother never broke down
after any of these deaths. She was the pillar of strength for the entire
family.

Her last sibling, a sister, passed five years after the death of my
father. Immediately after the passing of her last sibling, I saw my
mother break and almost cry for the first time. My mother told me
that being the last sibling was very difficult. She felt that she was alone
for the first time in her life. There was no connection left to her parents. The family cord was really broken and unable to be recreated. I
told my mother that she had her four children and 12 grandchildren
but she said that it was not the same.

Ten years have passed since my mother became, as she calls it, "an orphan." Most of those years were good. Twenty months ago my mother had kidney failure and was placed on dialysis. This, coupled with her blindness, high blood pressure and diabetes, made things difficult. Her health has continued to decline. She now has neuropathy in her feet. During this time period she has become a nonagenarian, and fights daily to keep her mind sharp. She will face bypass surgery in her right leg in a few short weeks. I know that she will fight to keep on living after this surgery.

The aging process is mystifying and sometimes hard to comprehend. I watch my mother continue to withstand the serious issues that life brings to her. She continues to be a fighter and a person who turns to God for her strength. She has great faith in her Lord and talks with him often in her times of need. The changes of life are inevitable but I have a wonderful role model in my mother.

Judy, school nurse

The Aging Process and Images Around Us

I've heard some people say that they can no longer change because time has taken a toll on their ability to do something differently or do it well. Others worry about whether they'll be seen as capable on their jobs as they grow older. Will I still be viewed as having fresh, creative ideas? Will my changing physical appearance affect my chances for a promotion, a romantic relationship or finding new friends?

The answers are directly linked to your perception of yourself. If you act confident at any age, that is what others will see and therefore believe. If you bring strong new ideas to the workplace, you'll be seen as effective. If you are sincere and treat yourself with respect, others will respect you, like you and want to be around you.

And when it comes to romance, ask yourself if feeling cared for and loved has anything to do with age. We have a need for human touch from infancy until the day that we die. We love to be loved, and age does not define what we feel in our hearts. Unfortunately, we often let our heads do all the talking, and tell ourselves that our worth is tied to our physical beauty.

The twists and turns of aging are going to happen whether we like it or not. This chapter is about how to embrace the process and face it in a way that allows you to thrive. Think of the metamorphosis of the butterfly. I chose the butterfly as a prominent symbol for *Life Changes* because it epitomizes transformation. These graceful beauties with colorful wings go through a complete metamorphosis: starting out as eggs, they develop into caterpillars, and then eventually emerge from cocoons as beautiful butterflies. Dave Steiger, an entomologist at the Insectarium in Philadelphia, says the fact that this metamorphosis even occurs is magical—that "an animal that is designed as a worm turns into a completely separate animal with wings."

We go through a metamorphosis of our own. Unlike the transformation of the butterfly, our human metamorphosis is a deepening of our inner beauty. This transformation is a testament to our strength and wisdom as we age and continue the lifelong process of growth. We are constantly learning incredible lessons that allow us to experience life with wisdom and a feeling of abundance. Physically, our bodies are growing older, but spiritually we are living a much fuller life, one with more depth, self awareness and understanding.

Our beauty is layers deep as we emerge from our own "cocoons" at every stage—teens, twenties, forties, sixties, seventies and beyond. The butterfly is known for its grace and splendor. We too are examples of that grace and splendor with each passing day, month and year, as we use what we've learned along the way to navigate our future.

Cosmetic Surgery and the Changing Face of Beauty

Now ask yourself what the ideal of beauty means to you. Do you feel more like the butterfly or the caterpillar at this point on your journey? As you think this over, consider some recent statistics on plastic surgery in America—a method of physical transformation that is becoming more and more commonplace.

The number of cosmetic plastic surgery procedures
increased five percent from 2003 to 2004, with more than
9.2 million procedures performed—a growth rate steady with
that of the US economy, according to statistics released by the
American Society of Plastic Surgeons. Five-year trending data
shows cosmetic procedures are up 24 percent from 2000.[*]

This statistic caught my eye as I've watched a number of shows that give us an operating-room view of patients seeking to transform their appearance. I felt there was more to find out about the people who pursue such measures and the doctors who work with them, so I sought the insights of one of these specialists—Dr. Anthony Griffin, star of ABC's hit television series *Extreme Makeover*. He was kind enough to share his views about body image and the fear of aging in an interview about the growing popularity of plastic surgery.

So why are women as well as men so fixated on trying to maintain their youthful looks? Dr. Griffin doesn't think people are obsessed. He instead attributes the popularity of cosmetic surgery to increased media exposure to the youthful ideal, and the current ease of obtaining procedures that would previously have been out of reach. "It's always been around," he says, "and in the past it's only been accessible to celebrities or very wealthy individuals. But now, because of the explosion of technology and the increase in discretionary income, a lot of people are able to afford these procedures."

Still, aren't people genuinely afraid to age, and what does this say about our society and our self-images? The doctor who operates on many of the most visible people in Hollywood had a stark response to this question. "I do a lot of high-end folks here in film and television and I can tell you that it is a devastating thing to age. Most actresses, most people in television know the demands of the media. They know that it's hard to have had that picture-perfect image and then to gradually lose it."

Dr. Griffin echoed the view that ten percent of people influence ninety percent of mass media. As a coach, however, I remind clients that despite the weight of social pressure, it is essential that they make choices that are truly best for them. Most importantly, we must understand *why* we're making particular decisions. Whether you choose to wear your hair

---

[*] The American Society of Plastic Surgeons, press release, March 15, 2005.

a certain way, lose weight, wear stylish clothes or undergo cosmetic surgery, the decision is entirely up to you.

Exterior changes will not automatically heal feelings of inadequacy or a lack of self-confidence. Whatever choices you make to enhance your appearance, make your mind and spirit a priority, too, by transforming yourself from the inside out. Dr. Griffin agrees with this philosophy, and adds that he actually declines a significant number of requests for surgery from people who have unrealistic expectations for the results. "You definitely have to do the inside work—there's no question about that. I'm always trying to find out if potential patients are happy with themselves." It's great to look good on the outside; just make sure you feel comfortable with yourself on the inside as well.

The Beauty In You

The beautiful butterfly is *inside* you, not just a societal idea of external physical beauty. The beauty in your transformation is that you know more today than you knew the day before. That's what aging with grace is all about. Through this process you grow more powerful and thus more beautiful, rich and strong from the inside out.

Notice the parallels in our own lives to that of the butterfly. I look at these lovely little creatures and I am captivated by them. There is something lyrical about the way they move as if to flirt with me in my garden. But what also fascinates me is the fact that they aren't seen as beautiful or captivating in the early stages of their lives.

The bugs that become butterflies end up as completely different animals at the end of their metamorphosis. How many of us feel this way about our own transformation? Some of us begin our lives feeling shy or inadequate and morph into confident, well-spoken men and women. I was always the chubby kid. Embracing an ideal of how I was "supposed to" look could have been very damaging. But my parents focused on who I was rather than how I looked. How many of us can look back now and see that we were much like the humble caterpillar that blossomed into the beautiful butterfly?

I love this analogy because, like the butterfly, we too need time to cocoon—to put a protective covering around ourselves while we develop and grow. No matter what we look like or feel like when we go into this cocoon, we can emerge from it as stronger, more capable individuals. Our beauty is measured not by looks but by our ability to overcome struggles and change our lives.

Think of the changes you can make when you're cocooning. You can heal, restore, care for and protect yourself in a powerful way. You may have a timeframe for change that requires you to insulate yourself from negative influences. Cocooning can allow you the time and space to nurture your spirit back to health.

We were cocooned in our mother's wombs—nourished and sheltered. There are times when we must take similar measures as adults, to wrap ourselves in a positive atmosphere. Taking the time to nest and think over your life changes allows you to make yourself a priority.

Before this chapter wraps up I'd like you to try an easy exercise to help boost your self-esteem. The next time you stand in the mirror, staring at yourself in an effort to fix something about your hair or makeup, take a few extra moments to admire the things that you like about yourself instead. Is it your warm brown eyes, welcoming smile or heart-shaped face? As we grow the key is to love ourselves from the inside out—to continue to appreciate our special attributes as time passes.

Embrace your inner beauty. At every stage of your life, walk with your head held high. Remember that age is a gift that doesn't have to be given. And the next time someone asks you how old you are, remind them that age isn't a number but a state of mind.

The Transformation—
When Change Works

As we learned in Chapter Seven, we can change our clothes, change the color of our hair and change the way we look. All of these are personal choices. However, working on yourself from the inside out is one of the best things you can do to make positive changes permanent. Internalizing your goals is just as essential. As you transform your life, it's up to you to make your changes as public or private as you'd like. Like the makeovers we see on TV, yours can be shared with an audience of friends who applaud you for being your personal best. Or it can be as private as the satisfaction that you'll feel when you reread the notes in your journal and see the progress you've made.

"The Knock at My Door"

Taylor, a pharmaceutical salesperson,
says church was an impetus for change in her life.

As a child growing up, I always had a sharing and caring heart for others. Somewhere along my life journey, the meaning of my vision in life was lost. Not until several years ago at a class on Praise and Worship at the Jericho City of Praise Church did I realize what was about to change my destiny and reroute me on my journey to enrich others.

As I listened to others pour out the trials and tribulations that had occurred in their lives, I was shocked and amazed to see that my situations were only trivial compared to theirs. Others' tragedies seemed greater than the small crises that had occurred in my life. As we began to get further into the lessons, my focus began to shift from my concerns to their concerns.

The class renewed my caring and sensitive spirit to focus on putting others' needs first. This attitude has transformed into a new wave of trusting totally in God to supply my family's needs when I gave to others. I lost my vision somewhere along my journey—letting work, my troubles and family problems get in the way of what I'm here on this earth to do. Thanks to God, he led me back, and I took the time to listen and heard the knock at my door to start meeting the needs of others.

Taylor, pharmaceutical salesperson

When change is working in your life it's because you're being flexible rather than so rigid that time moves along but you're standing still. This is the stage when you're going to be able to "reframe" situations.

Reframe: to see a situation in a different way.

Reshaping Your Life

I want you to try this: make your index finger and thumb on each hand into an "L" shape. Keeping your fingers like this, allow the thumbs to touch so that you can see through your hands as if you're looking through a window. Focus on something while looking through that "frame" you've made. Now put your arms down and look at the same object. You can see how looking at the same thing through the frame lets you focus squarely on it. Looking at the same object without the frame opens up a wider but less focused view.

I use this example in live audiences because with my hands down I see a sweeping crowd of three thousand people—but when I "reframe" I can see individual faces. Think about how this concept can help you to zero in on exactly what you desire to change. Is it something so big that perhaps you're missing the main issue that needs to be addressed?

I tell people in those audiences that there's no time like the present to change. Do it today. You don't need to make "resolutions" that surface only at the start of the new year. That's because resolutions tend to be watered down, shortcut solutions to problems that require long-term changes. As soon as the ball drops in Times Square, many of these promises we make to ourselves have already been forgotten. On the other hand, through the process of journaling and asking ourselves directed questions, we give our brains and bodies a chance to absorb the commitment to lasting change. We're not just talking about it—we're working on it.

Consider each day a new way of looking at your life, similar to the way we look at the new year—as a fresh start to renew our perspective. I see this as a clean slate, a time to forge new opportunities, build on past successes and focus on new goals.

Here are some of the tips I share with women and men seeking advice on how to be empowered throughout the year.

1. A new year gives us the gift of what I call "a new day–a new way." What I'm talking about is a new way of opening our perspectives and our minds to people, places and moments—real-life exchanges that we took for granted in the past year. Now is the time to build on last year's good experiences and refocus on what works well.

2. Out with the old and in with the new! There is something to be said for putting aside the negative baggage that we all carry. Maybe it's relationships we've neglected, health issues, poor work performance or bad spending habits. Dig deep. Ask yourself what works well as you go through the year and look to move forward.

3. Be organized! I can't say it enough. Organizational skills are essential as we seek to get our spiritual, mental, physical and financial houses in order. None of this is easy. Focus on one area at a time. As I always tell people, we are more than just our titles and what we do. Look at your life as a circle with integral parts—family, friends, home, career. Be determined in making sure all the pieces work together for a purposeful life!

Count on it—when the New Year rolls around there's a feeling that the previous year went too fast, that time was wasted or that we didn't accomplish everything we wanted to. With that in mind, do you see your New Year's "glass" as half empty or half full? If it's half empty, then perhaps you're only seeing–and therefore *feeling*–half the joy that awaits you. If you see your New Year's glass as half full, that's good. You're probably feeling that there's room to grow, explore and change. This outlook shifts our energy to the positive possibilities that await us.

Now, pause here for a moment. Take a few moments to close your eyes, take a deep breath and count to ten. While you're breathing, think about the positive and powerful aspects of your own life. See your personal vision. Think about what you've accomplished this week and what you want to achieve in the next one to see the power of change in your life. Whether it's happening at this very moment or not—by envisioning it in your mind, it becomes reality rather than mere fantasy.

Getting Rid of Your Gremlins

Now, each week prepare to make some amazing life changes. And don't let those little mental "gremlins" distract you.

Gremlins: the negative "I" statements that hold us back.

My gremlins tell me that I'm not tall enough or fit enough. These are dangerous little creatures when we allow them to creep in and dampen our enthusiasm or self-confidence. All of a sudden we doubt ourselves, our looks or what we're capable of. We can't completely exterminate these gremlins like they do in the movies. But we can train ourselves to change our thinking—"I'm *not* good enough" becomes "I *am* good enough."

Finally, when we're exercising change we have to know when to move on. This thought is very special to me because it came from my young son when he was a newly minted second grader. To say that this little story has changed my life is an understatement.

It was a regular day, filled with homework and activities like any other. I was driving and my son was in the back seat. I had been worrying about my parents' health—life as I knew it seemed to be rapidly unraveling. I was pretty quiet, and that was unusual for me. We stopped at a light and all of a sudden I heard my son blurt out, "You know, Mom, sometimes you just have to know when to move on!" A bit shocked, I said, "What do you mean by that?" What I was really thinking was, is this another thing they're now teaching in school? Then he went on to say, "Just let things go. Sometimes you really have to try new things."

After I picked my bottom jaw up off the floor, I asked him when he had followed his own advice. I mean after all, I'm the certified coach here! He went on to tell me that he did it all the time, especially when he played football. He had scored about eight touchdowns that season and had a pair of legs that could run as fast as the wind. "What is it you do when you're on the field?" I asked. He told me that he "never looks back." By simply continuing to move and never looking back–even when opposing players were trying to pull him down and grab his face mask and tear at his jersey–he kept looking ahead. He said, "If I look back I can't keep my eye on making the touchdown, and if I look back I won't make it to my goal."

The brilliance of this story is that nothing is more fundamental and honest than a message of hope from a child. So take it from Josh as you seek to make your own "touchdowns" this year: Never look back.

Chapter 9

A Final Word on Embracing Change

Writing this book was a milestone for me on my personal life journey. It took place at a time when I was going through tremendous changes. The loss of beloved friends and family and the onset of illness nearly kept me frozen in time. That's until I realized that all of these things are part of our journey—not just bad moments in time. It's these events that teach us to value our lives and our loved ones with a depth that we perhaps never could have imagined. The changes that threatened to break me down and eat away at my spirit never succeeded, because each time there was darkness there was also light. Every painful day was followed by a day of joy.

My dad has a saying that serves as a valuable reminder: "There are no good days or bad days, there's just life." It's how we handle the challenges that shows us the stuff we're made of. If you're trying to force yourself to change something but aren't getting closer to your goal, ask yourself why it is that nothing has noticeably changed. Think about whether the time is right for this new direction. Are you forcing your way into something that you're not adequately prepared for? Perhaps it's a great opportunity but the timing isn't right, or perhaps a better opportunity is just around the corner and God has a bigger plan. Sometimes we force change on ourselves rather than letting it evolve, even though we know deep inside that it's not the best thing for us.

When you're seeking change, feel with your heart and think with your head—use all that your body, mind and spirit are telling you, as well as all the knowledge and experiences you have had. So often we want to rush change rather than cultivate it. Perhaps you want to move to a new city or start an entirely different career. Sounds exciting, but how carefully have you thought this through? What is your plan for making these changes the most beneficial and long lasting they can be? I want you to take away the thought that change is one of the most effective tools we have in waking up to a clean slate every day.

"Riding the Wave of Change"

As Theresa tells us, with each day she is learning
more and more to lighten up and live in the moment.

I'm such a creature of habit and routines, I probably could live forever with the status quo, but of course that can't happen. I've really had to learn to go with the flow and not fight change. I guess the wave of changes for me started when I got married. I had dated the same man for several years and marriage was the next step, but still a change. Since getting married seven years ago, we bought a house, had two children, outgrew the house and just closed on a bigger one. Now, this is a natural course of events for a newly married couple. But, in the same period of time my company went through several mergers. I have six different business cards with different company names. As a part of these mergers I had to downsize staff, train the staff that survived the cuts—and at the same time my office relocated, my ten-minute commute was gone and I had to change my daughter's daycare.

This was a shock to my system! I have to say what got me through all of this was my relationships with my husband, boss and direct reports. The foundations I laid with these relationships were solid.

And with the added stability of family and friends I was able to ride the wave! I find the more change I experience, the better I am able to adapt. Just to let you know how far I've come—every Sunday night I used to lay out my clothes for the entire week. Now, I wake up in the morning and decide then and there what to wear. It's a good thing I've come so far because our CEO is resigning and we're up for sale—again!

Theresa, human resources executive

Change as a Cleanser

Change is a kind of cleansing—an incredible blessing that we are given with each breath. Every second that we're alive is an opportunity to evolve or choose a different direction, and that in itself is powerful. Recognize, too, that what worked at one point in your life may not have the same effects later on. Your likes and dislikes, your views and even deeply held beliefs may alter. How many times as a teenager did you say to yourself, if I have kids I'll *never* make them wash the dishes, keep their rooms clean, come home by midnight? But before we can even blink we've become adults and we have children of our own—and that curfew seems to make a lot more sense.

Being open to change creates so many possibilities for us. It allows us to forge new paths in our lives because we're able to weigh options that we might not have considered before. Opening our minds to see someone else's point of view helps us to move beyond longstanding arguments, even if we just agree to disagree. Allowing change into our lives makes us more flexible, so that when we hit bumps in the road we are not frozen in time.

So—fear not. Instead, imagine what the world would look like without change. No change of the seasons, no growth, development, maturity. Imagine if we weren't able to know more tomorrow than we do today. Embrace change and recognize it as *your* season to begin something refreshing and new, a time to work on you. I know that change is not easy. That's exactly why I decided to write on this subject. Our attitude toward change has such a far-reaching impact on how we live our lives—whether we turn away from opportunities out of fear or jump at the chance to enrich ourselves.

I have seen incredible transition and transformation on my own journey. This evolution would not have happened if I hadn't learned to embrace change. I, too, resisted at first, saying to myself, "Things are fine the way they are." But then I started to see that there was an even bigger plan and purpose for me. I had the opportunity to use all of my experiences as a newswoman, writer and producer–as well as a daughter, mother, wife and coach–to build a career sharing my inspiration for personal and professional success.

Use this book. Reread it when you need help seeing your way through a rough situation, and use it when change is joyful and exciting. *Life Changes* will help you develop a plan for preserving positive change. This approach can be especially useful for you as the seasons change. Think about the goals and changes you can make in the spring, summer, fall and winter. Applaud yourself for sustaining positive changes through each of the phases of the year.

I've designed this book as a life-changing tool that is relevant to your experiences. Be creative and delve into areas where change packs a powerful punch for you. These areas will likely include relationships, jobs and careers, finances, and the health of your mind, body and spirit.

Taking Charge of Change In Your Life

The goal is to take charge of change in your own life. Don't wait for someone else to change it for you. No one is going to find you a better job or put money in your bank account or truly take better care of you than you are. So change your thinking, develop a plan and change the way you're living! Use the professional coaching techniques and questions that I've outlined in this book, as well as the tools including my Phases of Change, Instruments/Agents of Change and the Three I's—intuition, instinct and inner voice. Empowering and lasting changes will come.

Know that:

Change is powerful and positive rather than negative.

You can learn how to be *proactive* rather than *reactive* when it comes to change.

The power to change is in your hands.

Embracing change even during difficult times can greatly improve the quality of your life.

The final section of this book is your *Life Changes Journal.* Using this journal effectively requires that you be honest with yourself about the changes that are occurring and the changes that you'd like to make. Look deeply into your motivations for specific changes. Is this change what *you* really want, or is it what someone else thinks is good for you? Are you being authentic, honest and kind to yourself? Is this a positive change—and one that you're truly committed to? Explore the questions carefully, and congratulate yourself for taking on change!

Your Life Changes Journal

I designed this wonderful journaling section with you in mind. Open your heart, your mind and your spirit to the power of change. Use it along with *Life Changes* and advance your understanding of the changes that are occurring at this very moment, the changes that are heading your way and the changes that have made a tremendous difference in your life journey thus far.

As I tell my clients, I coach them by meeting them where they are today. A journal is something very special. It is a way to express yourself and learn more about your journey day by day. Take the time to use it, answering carefully the questions in *Life Changes* and the open-ended questions below. Through your responses, you'll begin to see larger solutions taking shape. We all have the answers within us; we just need help bringing them to the surface. That's the purpose of *Life Changes* and your *Life Changes Journal*.

Your goals and the changes you want to make can be different from week to week or you can work on a single change over a 52-week period. Remember, this is *your* journal. There are no right or wrong answers. You're allowing yourself to grow and develop by exploring the possibilities that await you through change.

At the end of this section, you'll see a Life Changes Pledge that will encourage the positive energy you've already put forth in allowing all this information to flow through you and around you. Take the pledge and meet the change to develop a wonderful life you love.

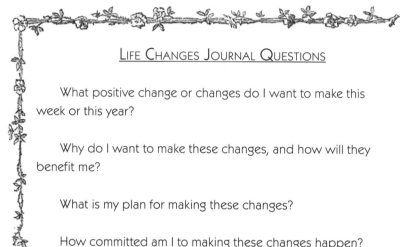

LIFE CHANGES JOURNAL QUESTIONS

What positive change or changes do I want to make this week or this year?

Why do I want to make these changes, and how will they benefit me?

What is my plan for making these changes?

How committed am I to making these changes happen?

What have I done this week, this month or this year to move toward a specific goal?

How has change been visible in my life today?

What can I learn from a new experience I've had recently? How can I use it to my benefit?

If I am dissatisfied with a change that is happening in my life, what can I do about it?

52-Week Life Changes Journal

WEEK 1

Faith

Faith

Effective change is
about faith—believing in
what I cannot see.

**W
E
E
K
1**

W E E K 2

Hope

Hope

Effective change is about
hope—knowing even in
my darkest hours that
there will be better days.

WEEK 2

WEEK

3

Focus

Focus

Effective change is about focus—removing the clutter in my mind to zero in on what really matters.

W E E K 3

WEEK 4

Clarity

Clarity

Effective change is about
clarity—seeing through a
situation from the inside out
rather than the outside in.

WEEK 4

WEEK 5

Joy

Joy

Effective change is about
joy—the spark in my heart
that translates to my head
with euphoric delight.

WEEK 5

WEEK

6

Determination

Determination

Effective change is about
determination—moving
ahead without fear in the
face of challenges.

WEEK

7

Endurance

Endurance

Effective change is
about endurance—going
the extra step when I think
I've given all I've got.

W
E
E
K

7

WEEK 8

Excitement

Excitement

Effective change is about
excitement—stepping outside
the ordinary to relish an emotion
that only I can measure.

WEEK 8

WEEK 9

Sensitivity

Sensitivity

Effective change is about
sensitivity—using my compassion
and thoughtful emotions
to understand others.

WEEK 9

W
E
E
K

10

Prosperity

Prosperity

Effective change is about prosperity—realizing that small investments in me grow into big life-changing gains.

**W
E
E
K

10**

WEEK

11

Abundance

Abundance

Effective change is about abundance—measuring the fruits of my efforts in terms of what I've shared with others.

WEEK

11

WEEK 12

Serenity

Serenity

Effective change is about
serenity—the calmness I maintain
inside no matter how turbulent
the world is around me.
I maintain it. I own
it and I control it.

**W
E
E
K**

12

**W
E
E
K

13**

Peace

Peace

Effective change is about
peace—finding my center,
the place where I love to be.

**W
E
E
K

13**

WEEK 14

Perseverance

Perseverance

Effective change is about
perseverance—transforming
pain into progress to reach
new heights in my life.

WEEK 14

**W
E
E
K**

15

Happiness

Happiness

Effective change is about
happiness—the involuntary
reflex that makes me
smile with delight.

WEEK 15

WEEK 16

Depth

Depth

Effective change is about
depth—exposing myself
to new opportunities that
affect me at a deep level.

**W
E
E
K
16**

**W
E
E
K**

17

Maturity

Maturity

Effective change is about
maturity—charting my own
course by taking responsibility
for where I want to go and
what I want to do.

**W
E
E
K

17**

WEEK 18

Discernment

Discernment

Effective change is about
discernment—the inner voice
of judgment that guides me to
make successful decisions
during times of change.

**W
E
E
K

18**

**W
E
E
K

19**

Kindness

Kindness

Effective change is about
kindness—an open heart,
an open mind, two open ears
and one soft-spoken tongue.

WEEK 19

WEEK

20

Fortitude

Fortitude

Effective change is about fortitude—the ability to stand tall with courage and steely determination.

WEEK 20

W
E
E
K

21

Control

Control

Effective change is about
control—exercising my better
judgment over my free will
in a world where there
are so many choices.

**W
E
E
K

21**

**W
E
E
K

22**

Balance

Balance

Effective change is about balance—a harmonious arrangement that is pleasing to me in mind, body and spirit.

WEEK 22

WEEK

23

Consciousness

Consciousness

Effective change is about
consciousness—awareness of
what's around me, the people I
meet, the experiences I have.

WEEK 23

WEEK

24

Restoration

Restoration

Effective change is about
restoration—rejuvenating
my very core in order to
face new struggles.

WEEK 24

**W
E
E
K

25**

Vision

Vision

Effective change is about
vision—a transparency
of the soul that is realized
through my eyes and
touches hearts.

W E E K 25

W
E
E
K

26

imagination

Imagination

Effective change is about imagination—the freedom of thought that fuels my dreams, goals and aspirations.

WEEK 26

WEEK

27

Creativity

Creativity

Effective change is about creativity—working with the gifts that are uniquely mine.

W
E
E
K

27

**W
E
E
K**

28

Desire

Desire

Effective change is about desire—the passion inside me that generates positive movement in my life.

WEEK

28

WEEK

29

Growth

Growth

Effective change is about
growth—knowing that every
day I am further ahead
in my life's journey.

**W
E
E
K

29**

WEEK

30

Support

Support

Effective change is about support—having the maturity to seek a safety net that makes me stronger and more capable.

WEEK 30

W
E
E
K

31

Survival

Survival

Effective change is about survival—continuing to live, feel and grow while banning bitterness from my heart.

WEEK 31

**W
E
E
K

32**

Intuition

Intuition

Effective change is about intuition—following a higher state of awareness to tune in to the things that can benefit me.

WEEK 32

W
E
E
K

33

Renewal

Renewal

Effective change is about renewal—replenishing the energy source deep within my body to strengthen me for the journey ahead.

W E E K

33

WEEK

34

Organization

Organization

Effective change is about
organization—putting the things
I value in order and making sure
they have a place in my life.

WEEK
34

WEEK 35

Connecting

Connecting

Effective change is about
connecting—touching someone
deeply through my words
and actions.

WEEK 35

WEEK

36

Teaching

Teaching

Effective change is about
teaching—sharing what
I know, and learning
in the process.

WEEK

36

W E E K

37

Planning

Planning

Effective change is about planning—preparing myself for the experiences I have yet to encounter and the places I have yet to go.

W
E
E
K

38

Persistence

Persistence

Effective change is about persistence—the natural drive within my body that is unwilling to give up or succumb to negativity.

WEEK 38

**W
E
E
K**

39

Curiosity

Curiosity

Effective change is about
curiosity—remembering the
child inside me that wants to
explore and discover new things.

**W
E
E
K**

39

WEEK

40

Laughter

Laughter

Effective change is about
laughter—the joy of seeing
the humor in my life and the
missteps I take as I hit some
bumps along the way.

**W
E
E
K

40**

W E E K

41

Assurance

Assurance

Effective change is about
assurance—making a pledge
to myself that I can do
anything I put my mind to.

W
E
E
K

41

W E E K

42

Tranquility

Tranquility

Effective change is about
tranquility—using stillness
to my benefit, to evoke the
calm, quiet side of me.

WEEK 42

**W
E
E
K**

43

Resilience

Resilience

Effective change is about
resilience—using the
strength of my will to
get back up when I've
been knocked down.

W
E
E
K

43

WEEK 44

Attitude

Attitude

Effective change is about
attitude—capitalizing on
my talents and knowing
why they're important to
the world around me.

WEEK 44

W
E
E
K

45

Gratitude

Gratitude

Effective change is about
gratitude—being thankful for
the small things in life.

**W
E
E
K

45**

W E E K

46

Deliverance

Deliverance

Effective change is about
deliverance—liberating myself
from thoughts that hold me back
from reaching my true potential.

WEEK 46

W E E K

47

Wisdom

Wisdom

Effective change is about
wisdom—recognizing that I
have knowledge and insight
and acknowledging that I'm
smart enough to use them.

WEEK 47

**W
E
E
K

48**

Strategy

Strategy

Effective change is about strategy—devising an action plan that shapes my life into what I want it to be.

WEEK 48

W
E
E
K

49

Communication

Communication

Effective change is about
communication—being as good as
listener as I am a talker as I exchange
thoughts, ideas and information.

WEEK

49

W E E K

50

Enlightenment

Enlightenment

Effective change is about enlightenment—
the light that shines within me when I see
myself reach a new level of clarity.

WEEK 50

W
E
E
K

51

Humility

Humility

Effective change is about
humility—knowing when to
ask for help and using the
guidance I'm given.

**W
E
E
K

51**

WEEK

52

Grace

Grace

Effective change is about
grace—breathing in the beauty
of each day with a thankful word,
thought or deed that allows me
to be kind and loving to myself.

WEEK 52

My Life Changes Power Pledge

This is your Life Changes Power Pledge. Repeat it daily to remind yourself of the strength that lies within you always, no matter what changes revolve around you. To pledge to change your life for the better is to make one of the greatest commitments a person can make. Seeing through the changes that attempt to 'block your blessings' is a way to overcome adversity. Pledge that you'll make a difference to yourself in a powerful way!

MY LIFE CHANGES POWER PLEDGE

I, (say your name), pledge to embrace change because I know that without it I can't grow to my fullest potential.

I pledge to learn from the changes that I have already gone through and to use that knowledge to improve myself daily.

I pledge to see change through a different set of eyes, putting fear, guilt and worry aside when life takes an unexpected turn.

I pledge to be positive, opening myself to the new possibilities and opportunities that I am destined to encounter.

I pledge to face difficult changes by channeling my positive energy toward the future rather than languishing in negative thoughts of the past.

I pledge to develop a plan that allows me to take control of my life and make positive changes to live a life that I love.

Afterword

An afterword is a way to bring the reader that last bit of information you'd like them to know. I thought long and hard about writing this afterword and the same thought kept coming into my mind: that no matter what happens to us or around us, we hold within us the power to change. As I've said throughout this book, a fresh opportunity for change comes each and every second, with each and every breath.

It is simply never too late to change our views, change the way we eat, change the way we communicate or behave. It is never too late to try something different, to meet someone new, to change a relationship by mending fences or saying you're sorry. When you remove animosity and anger, the relationship has changed—no matter how the other person reacts. You have shifted negative energy into positive territory and altered the dynamics of the situation. Try arguing with someone who won't argue back—it's pretty tough.

Know that you can change your job, and more importantly, your outlook on the job you have now. Chart your own course for success. Seek the promotion or new position that will offer you the things you feel you deserve and desire. But if you can't change your job physically, change it mentally. In fact, it's often the mental changes that have the most impact. It means a lot to have mental freedom, to see things in a new way, to release the things that seem wrong and instead focus on what is right. That's where mental freedom equals power.

Know that you can change your spirit. There is nothing more devastating than a broken spirit. But you have the power to invigorate your spirit and change your life.

I often think about the sports my children have played and the teams they've tried out for. It has sometimes been tough to watch their spirits fall when they didn't succeed in the way they'd hoped. Even as they've become good athletes it hasn't been easy. They know what it's like to try hard but still not make the starting lineup. Transforming the negative or sad energy into energy that is positive and uplifting requires them to look inside themselves and change the way they view the situation. I remind them to tell themselves, "I'm sitting the bench today, but by just being present, by competing and working to the best of my ability, I'm already a winner." When you're challenging yourself and doing something you love, how can you lose?

And finally, know that this life is about *your* metamorphosis. We all start out as little caterpillars exploring what the world has to offer. We develop our own beauty and grace through transformation. What truly changes us into the beautiful butterflies that we are at heart is our life experience, both good and bad. It is experience that leads to enlightenment, and yes, these lessons often come after a bout with a tough situation.

Thank you for allowing me to be your guide on this leg of your journey. God bless and be well.

So like the beautiful butterfly I spread my wings.
Gracefully and gently I take flight. I land where I am
nourished, basking in the warm summer sun. I let my
admirers know not to be fooled by my gentle appearance,
for behind it lie unimaginable strength and determination.

–Jennifer Lewis-Hall

About the Author

Sharing with others how to live well and "enjoy the journey" is the mission of network journalist, certified life coach, motivational speaker and author Jennifer Lewis-Hall. It's how she has built a thriving career while being a dedicated wife, a mother of two sons and a friend to many. *Life Changes* is her second book, following the highly acclaimed *Life's a Journey–Not a Sprint*.

A recognized expert on relationships, work and lifestyle issues, Lewis-Hall is a frequent keynote speaker at major corporate events, business organization conferences, women's groups, and civic and community associations. She has appeared on the *Today* show and in the pages of *O, The Oprah Magazine*, and as a professionally trained and certified life coach she has been featured on *Lifetime Radio*. Previously, as a contributor on WCBS-TV in New York and a correspondent on CNBC Business News, Lewis-Hall provided in-depth market reporting and covered the anchor desk for internationally televised NBC network programs including *Early Today* and *The Wall Street Journal Report*.

Jennifer Lewis-Hall loves to inspire women and men wherever she travels. In addition to her roles as a speaker and journalist, she is the creator of Be Open To Grace™ Products, which includes a line of inspirational cards licensed by American Greetings. She holds a master's degree in Journalism from Northwestern University's Medill School of Journalism and a bachelor's degree in Economics and Finance from Douglass College at Rutgers University. The recipient of numerous awards and honors, she is an elected member of the Rutgers African-American

Alumni Alliance Hall of Fame and the Douglass Society at Rutgers University for outstanding achievement in the field of journalism. She lives in New Jersey with her husband and two children.

Speaking Engagements
and Ordering *Life Changes*

Contact Jennifer Lewis-Hall through her website:

www.jenniferlewishall.com

Speaking Events, Keynotes and Coaching: I'm fortunate enough to continue my career in television and tour the country speaking to large audiences, addressing corporate groups and coaching. You can reach me through my website for corporate speaking events, keynote addresses, panel engagements, or coaching and consulting.

Share Your Story: I'm always delighted to hear from people who have evolved positively through the power of change—especially after reading *Life Changes*. Please share your story with me by contacting me through my website.

To order *Life Changes*, please go to www.jenniferlewishall.com, www.amazon.com or a bookstore near you.

Bulk purchase discounts available.

The Journey Productions, LLC
Metuchen, New Jersey 08840